W9-AWO-293

ALSO BY STAN MACK

*Real Life American Revolution*
*Ten Bears in My Bed*
*Hard Time* (with Janet Bode)

# THE STORY OF THE JEWS

# STAN MACK

# THE STORY OF THE JEWS

## A 4,000-YEAR ADVENTURE

VILLARD

NEW YORK

Copyright © 1998 by Stan Mack

All rights reserved under International and Pan-American Copyright
Conventions. Published in the United States by Villard Books, a
division of Random House, Inc., New York, and simultaneously in
Canada by Random House of Canada Limited, Toronto.

VILLARD BOOKS is a registered trademark of Random House, Inc.

This work was originally published in hardcover
by Villard Books, a division of Random House, Inc.

Library of Congress Cataloging-in-Publication Data

Mack, Stan.
The story of the Jews: a 4,000-year
adventure / Stan Mack.
p.    c.m.
ISBN 0-375-75336-2
1. Jews—History—Comic books, strips, etc.   I. Title
DS118.M187   1997
909´.04924´002´07—dc21   97-24415

Random House website address: www.atrandom.com

*Printed in the United States of America on acid-free paper*

24689753

FIRST PAPERBACK EDITION

*To the families who make up my family—*
*Kamaiko, Hyman, Jacobs, and Mack—*
*and to all those who came before;*
*to my children, and to all those*
*who will come after,*
*I celebrate them.*

# ACKNOWLEDGMENTS

Most of my research came from books, articles, museums, and films. But I also turned to a number of people who generously offered their wisdom, expertise, experience, passion, and objectivity. I am indebted and grateful to the following people: Doreen Braverman, Linda Broessel, Lawrence Bush, Rabbi Melissa Crespy, Dr. Lisa Epstein, Dr. Marc Michael Epstein, Adria Frede, Marvin Gettleman, Itche Goldberg, Rabbi Lawrence Goldmark, Rabbi Marshall Hurwitz, Idaho Eights and Ron Fowler, Michael Kahan, Toni Kamaiko, Rabbi William Kloner, Joseph Kramer, M.D., Gail Kredenser Mack, Kenneth Mack (maps), Pearl Mack, Joe Mohbat, Lydia Neumann, Lillian Rabins, Rabbi John Rosove, Alysa Turkowitz, David Van Biema, Mark Wagner, Yulana Zahajkewycz, Rabbi Bernard M. Zlotowitz; and in Israel: the Angel family, Josef Chajes, Yaakov and Ruth Fogelman, David and Miriam Friedman, Daniel Gavron, Rabbi Hank Skirball, and Joee Teplitsky.

To my agent, Lew Grimes, for his faith in me and in this innovative project. To my editor, Melissa Milsten, who sure-handedly and safely guided me over, under, around, and through all the hazards of book production to a successful launch.

And finally, and most especially, to the one person without whose strength, understanding, assistance, and life-sustaining soups I could never have accomplished this undertaking, my partner, Janet Bode.

# CONTENTS

# INTRODUCTION

Welcome to the astonishing history of the Jews.

We'll begin our (sometimes irreverent) journey four thousand years ago near the Euphrates River when a wandering tribal chieftain named Abraham meets his God for the first time. And we'll be present at the foot of Mount Sinai when this same God makes his bargain with Moses. My narrative takes the view that, whether divine truth or myth, these events are part of our historical reality. It is the richness of faith and the depth of humanity found in their sacred and historical writings that may well be the most important contributions of the Jewish people.

We will walk with the Prophets, who pointed us toward a belief in one God and a respect for law, morality, and individual equality; we will meet Deborah, Alexandra, Beruriah, and other women representing the intellectual and nurturing strength of women in the Jewish culture; and we will travel with the ordinary Jews as they make their way through all the major currents of Western history. This is the story of the "People of the Book," who have taught us that there is purpose and meaning in everything, but who (as it is said), when you get three together, come up with ten opposing views.

I approached this project as a Jew who was uncertain of his own Jewishness and in the dark about most of Jewish history. When I was a child, my yeshiva-trained immigrant grandfather lived his last years in our house. Each day he would take his books and go off to synagogue to parley over the Talmud. I'm sorry now that he and I did not get to know each other better. As I began my research, I imagined him by my side, guiding my thoughts, and . . . uh . . . still scratching his head over my cartoons. For me, researching and writing this book was a personal journey into my own roots. For all those with a desire to connect, this is an exploration of who we are, how we got here, and the historical bond linking all Jews.

I have assumed a conceit: that I, a relative novice, could tell the four-thousand-year history of the Jews, and do it simply. And I recognize that the risks of simplification can be exaggeration, trivialization, and, God help me, error. As I leapt from century to century, I tried to follow the main streams of the Jewish experience. Some readers will find that their own heritage has been left out—and for that, I apologize.

As I sorted through the feast of research material, discovering and testing ideas, I fixed on a central theme. This is the story of a brave, resilient, tenacious people whose faith and talents shone through some very dark times. My aim was to present this extraordinary story well, encouraging the reader to view this book as a doorway into a huge world of further study.

A note about the form of the book: It is in a different language than the reader may be used to—not a traditional illustrated text, nor truly a comic strip, but with something of the conciseness of a political cartoon; definitely words and pictures meant to be read together—a cross between ancient illuminated manuscripts and a modern web page.

And for those who find fault, let us compare notes, invite a few more points of view to make it interesting, and debate, like the people we are.

# I

# GETTING THE MESSAGE

# 1

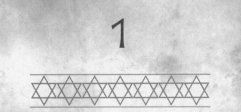

# THE
# INVISIBLE
# GOD

ABRAHAM–MOSES
2000 BCE–1200 BCE

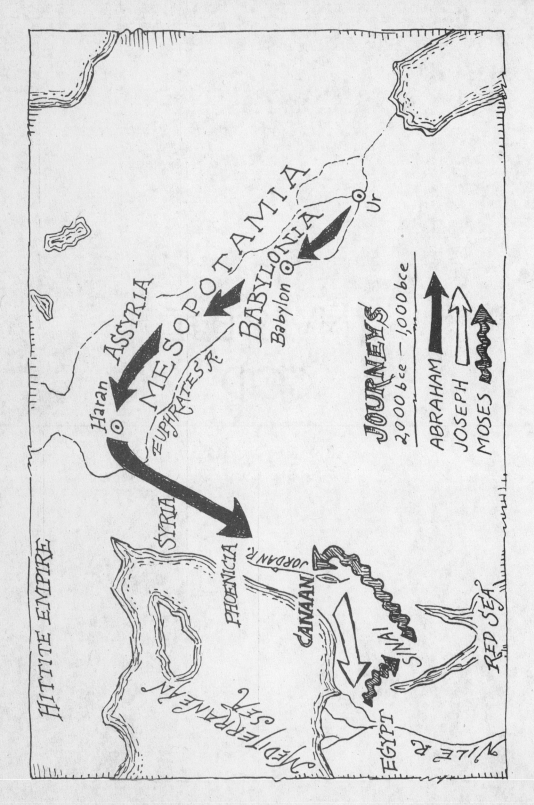

# ABOUT 4,000 YEARS AGO,

DURING THE BRONZE AGE, TRIBAL GROUPS CAME MARCHING OUT OF MESOPOTAMIA, HEADING WEST ACROSS THE EUPHRATES RIVER. <u>ACCORDING TO THE BIBLE, AMONG THEM WERE A CLAN-CHIEFTAIN,</u> ABRAHAM, AND HIS WIFE, SARAH.

WHILE STOPPING IN THE TOWN OF HARAN, **ABRAHAM MET HIS GOD FOR THE FIRST TIME.**

ABRAHAM

I HEAR SOMETHING.

LIKE WHAT?

THE BIBLE TELLS US THAT, THROUGH ABRAHAM, GOD DELIVERED TO THE WORLD THE CONCEPT OF MONOTHEISM, **THE BELIEF IN ONE SUPREME BEING.**

ABRAHAM, I AM THE ONE TRUE GOD, AND I HAVE CHOSEN YOU TO HELP ME MAKE THE WORLD A BETTER PLACE.

I EXPECT YOU TO LIVE UP TO THE HIGHEST MORAL STANDARDS, AND I WILL GIVE YOU AND YOUR DESCENDANTS THE LAND OF CANAAN FOREVER.

TRUE, YOU MAY SUFFER FOR YOUR BELIEFS, BUT IF YOU VIOLATE THIS COVENANT, YOU WILL BRING DOWN MY WRATH ON YOU.

ABRAHAM, DID GOD SAY HOW LONG THIS COVENANT WILL LAST?

HE SAID IT WAS FOREVER.

OY!

THE WORLD'S FIRST "OY!"

# AS A RESULT OF THESE ENCOUNTERS, JEWISH HISTORY WOULD COME TO RECOGNIZE ABRAHAM AS THE FATHER OF THE JEWISH PEOPLE, THE JEWS AS HAVING A SPECIAL RELATIONSHIP WITH GOD, AND ISRAEL AS THE PROMISED LAND.

## IN THOSE ANCIENT DAYS, PEOPLE BELIEVED THEIR LIVES WERE RULED BY MULTITUDES OF GODS. BUT THEIR GODS WERE UNTRUSTWORTHY AND BEHAVED IN A DEVILISHLY HUMAN FASHION. THE PEOPLE REPRESENTED THEIR GODS AS BOTH ANIMALS AND HUMANS.

**THE GOD OF THE JEWISH PEOPLE WOULD BE DIFFERENT.** HE WAS TRUSTWORTHY AND ULTIMATELY JUST. YOU COULD COUNT ON HIM. HE WAS THE GOD OF ALL HUMANITY. **HE WASN'T OF** THE WORLD. HE **CREATED** THE WORLD.

**THAT DOESN'T MEAN I'M NOT HERE!**

**BY HAVING ONE GOD OVER ALL,** THE WORLD COULD GET RID OF ALL THE SCANDALOUS BEHAVIOR THAT WENT ON AMONG THE PAGAN GODS. WITH ONE ETHICAL GOD, PEOPLE WOULD HAVE A GUIDE FOR STRENGTHENING THEIR OWN MORAL CHARACTER.

ABRAHAM AND SARAH FINALLY ARRIVED IN **CANAAN.** GOD HADN'T MENTIONED THAT TINY CANAAN WAS A CROSSROADS CONNECTING ASIA, AFRICA, AND EUROPE, AND USED BY GLORY-BOUND ARMIES AND FORTUNE-HUNTING TRADERS.

PROMISED LAND OR NOT, THIS IS ONE ROUGH PIECE OF REAL ESTATE!

PHOENICIA
EGYPT

SYRIA
ASSYRIA
BABYLONIA

ABRAHAM AND SARAH SETTLED DOWN. _VERY_ LATE IN LIFE THEY HAD A SON, ISAAC, WHO, WITH HIS WIFE, REBECCA, HAD A SON, JACOB. JACOB FATHERED TWELVE SONS, WHOSE FAMILIES WOULD SPREAD OUT, TAKING ON THE LOCAL TRIBES AND THEIR GODS.

Y'SEE, OUR GOD ISN'T REALLY FIGHTING YOUR GOD BECAUSE OUR GOD _IS_ YOUR GOD AND YOUR GOD ISN'T REALLY A GOD BECAUSE...

ALL RIGHT, ALL RIGHT, WHATEVER!

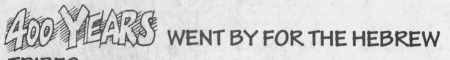 **WENT BY FOR THE HEBREW TRIBES.** THE BIBLE REPORTS THE FOLLOWING EVENTS FROM THOSE YEARS. FOR MORE DETAILS, READ THE **BOOK OF GENESIS.**

**ABRAHAM** FATHERED ANOTHER CHILD, **ISHMAEL**, WITH A SERVANT, HAGAR (SARAH WAS NOT AMUSED). ISHMAEL WOULD BECOME THE FATHER OF THE ARAB PEOPLE.

**SARAH**, AT 90, GAVE BIRTH TO **ISAAC**. GOD FIRST ORDERED ABRAHAM TO SACRIFICE ISAAC AND THEN, IN THE NICK OF TIME, GOD CHANGED HIS MIND.

**JACOB** HAD A FIGHT WITH AN ANGEL WHO NICKNAMED JACOB **ISRAEL**. JACOB'S DESCENDANTS WOULD BE CALLED THE **CHILDREN OF ISRAEL.**

**JOSEPH**, A SON OF JACOB AND **RACHEL**, WAS SOLD BY HIS ENVIOUS BROTHERS AND ENDED UP A SLAVE IN EGYPT.

ABOUT 1400 BCE, **JOSEPH**, A TALENTED GUY, TALKED HIS WAY OUT OF HIS CHAINS AND INTO A TOP JOB IN THE EGYPTIAN ROYAL COURT.

When hard times hit Canaan, many Israelites headed for the fertile Nile, where Joseph helped them get established. But when a new Pharaoh, Ramses II, went on a building binge, **ALL FOREIGNERS, INCLUDING THE ISRAELITES, WERE FORCED INTO SLAVE LABOR GANGS.**

AROUND 1300 bce, EGYPT BEGAN KILLING MALE ISRAELITE CHILDREN TO HALT THE ISRAELITES' GROWING NUMBERS. A MALE BABY WAS FOUND IN THE REEDS OF THE NILE BY PHARAOH'S DAUGHTER.

THE BABY, **MOSES,** WAS RAISED IN LUXURY. YET, AS A YOUTH, **HE WAS DEEPLY TROUBLED BY THE PAIN OF THE SLAVES.**

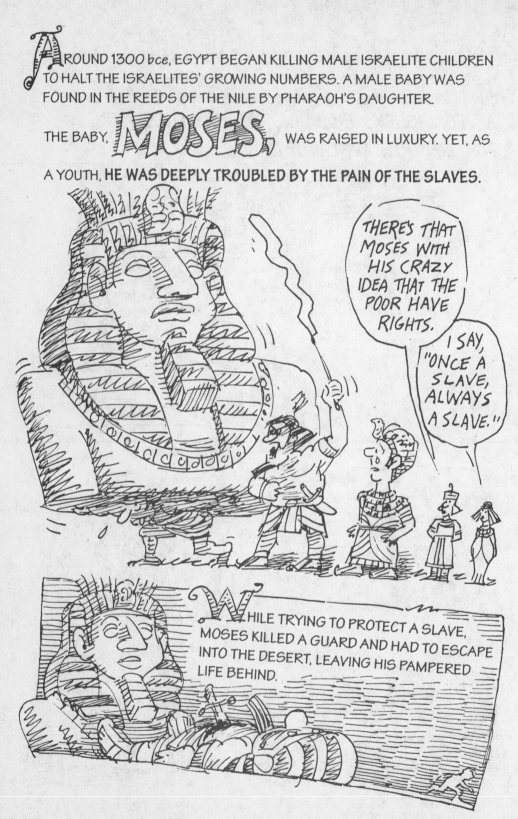

THERE'S THAT MOSES WITH HIS CRAZY IDEA THAT THE POOR HAVE RIGHTS.

I SAY, "ONCE A SLAVE, ALWAYS A SLAVE."

WHILE TRYING TO PROTECT A SLAVE, MOSES KILLED A GUARD AND HAD TO ESCAPE INTO THE DESERT, LEAVING HIS PAMPERED LIFE BEHIND.

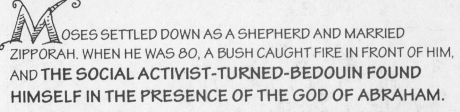

MOSES SETTLED DOWN AS A SHEPHERD AND MARRIED ZIPPORAH. WHEN HE WAS 80, A BUSH CAUGHT FIRE IN FRONT OF HIM, AND **THE SOCIAL ACTIVIST-TURNED-BEDOUIN FOUND HIMSELF IN THE PRESENCE OF THE GOD OF ABRAHAM.**

## GOD SPOKE TO A RELUCTANT MOSES.

WITH AARON'S HELP, MOSES CONVINCED THE ISRAELITES THAT IT WAS TIME TO BREAK OUT OF THEIR CAPTIVITY.

GOD SAID IF YOU DON'T LIKE SOMETHING, YOU CAN CHANGE IT THROUGH COLLECTIVE ACTION.

WITH EGYPT SUFFERING FROM A SERIES OF DISASTERS AND PLAGUES THAT LOOSED LOCUSTS, FROGS, FLIES, AND LICE ON THE LAND, **MOSES AND HIS BAND OF REBELS MADE THEIR ESCAPE.**

**M**IRACULOUSLY, THE WATERS OF THE **RED SEA** PARTED FOR MOSES, AARON, THEIR SISTER, MIRIAM, AND THE EX-SLAVES. THEN THE WATERS RUSHED IN AND ENGULFED THE PURSUING EGYPTIAN ARMY.

**T**ODAY, SCHOLARS SEARCH FOR HISTORICAL EVIDENCE FOR THE BIBLICAL ACCOUNT OF THE EXODUS.

IT WASN'T THE RED SEA, IT WAS THE MEDITERRANEAN.

NO, THE GULF OF SUEZ.

A VOLCANO IN THE AEGEAN.

A TIDAL WAVE.

IT WAS DIVINE BREATH.

ABOUT THIS MOMENTOUS EVENT, EGYPTIAN HISTORICAL RECORDS TELL US NOTHING.

MOSES LED HIS MUTINEERS INTO THE SINAI DESERT AND INTRODUCED THEM TO THEIR GOD. AROUND 1280 bce, ON **MOUNT SINAI,** HIDDEN BY HEAVY CLOUD COVER AND SURROUNDED BY SMOKE AND FLAME, <u>**GOD AND MOSES HELD A SERIES OF MEETINGS.**</u>

**A**ND WITH THOSE MEETINGS, GOD REAFFIRMED HIS COVENANT WITH THE CHILDREN OF ABRAHAM.

MOSES, TELL THE ISRAELITES THAT I LOVE THEM AND THAT THEIR JOB IS TO FOLLOW MY COMMANDMENTS AND CARRY THEM TO THE WORLD. IT WILL BE THEIR BURDEN AND THEIR GLORY. AND THEY WILL MULTIPLY AND PROSPER, AND CANAAN WILL BE THEIRS FOREVER.

**G**OD'S WORDS LINKED THE MYSTERY OF A DIVINE BEING WITH THE IDEAL OF JUSTICE AND MERCY FOR ALL. HE PRESENTED MORALS, ETHICS, AND LAWS FOR PEOPLE TO LIVE BY. HE GAVE TO MOSES A TOTAL OF 613 COMMANDMENTS. *HERE ARE THE FIRST TEN.*

I, ADONAI, AM YOUR GOD.

YOU MAY HAVE NO OTHER GODS IN PLACE OF ME.

YOU MAY NOT SWEAR FALSELY IN THE NAME OF GOD.

REMEMBER THE SABBATH DAY IN ORDER TO KEEP IT HOLY.

HONOR YOUR FATHER AND MOTHER.

YOU MUST NOT MURDER.

YOU MUST NOT COMMIT ADULTERY.

YOU MUST NOT STEAL.

YOU MUST NOT TESTIFY FALSELY AGAINST YOUR NEIGHBOR.

YOU MUST NOT DESIRE WHAT IS YOUR NEIGHBOR'S.

FOR 40 YEARS, IN THE SINAI, MOSES TRIED TO OVERCOME HIS PEOPLE'S DOUBTS ABOUT GOD. FINALLY, **CARRYING THE ARK THEY'D BUILT TO HOLD THEIR RADICAL NEW IDEAS,** THE WANDERERS HEADED FOR CANAAN.

WITH CANAAN IN VIEW, MOSES DIED. THE MAN WHO'D LED THE ISRAELITES OUT OF EGYPT WOULD NEVER SET FOOT IN THE PROMISED LAND. HE LEFT **JOSHUA,** THE ISRAELITES' FIRST GREAT GENERAL, IN CHARGE.

21

# 2

# THE EMPIRE BUILDERS

## (JOSHUA–SOLOMON)
### 1200 BCE–925 BCE

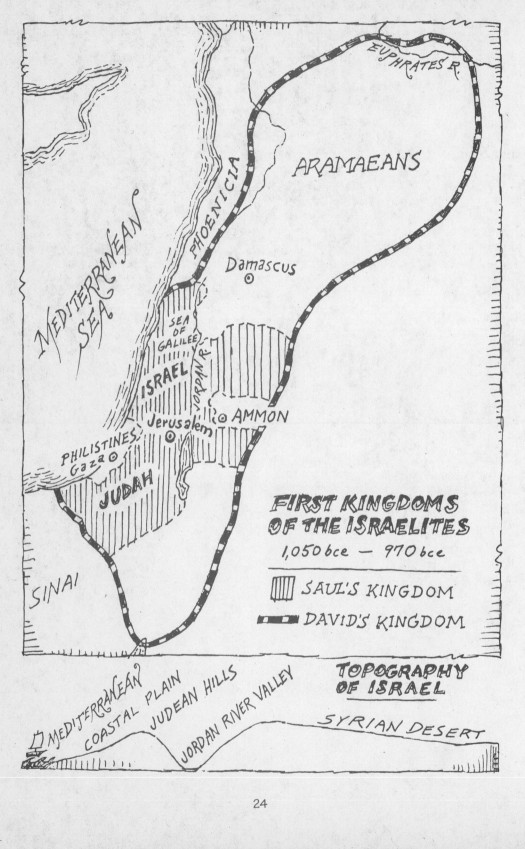

ARAMAEANS

MEDITERRANEAN SEA

PHOENICIA

EUPHRATES R.

Damascus

SEA OF GALILEE

JORDAN R.

ISRAEL

Jerusalem

AMMON

PHILISTINES
Gaza

JUDAH

SINAI

**FIRST KINGDOMS OF THE ISRAELITES**
1,050 bce — 970 bce

‖ SAUL'S KINGDOM
▬ ▬ DAVID'S KINGDOM

**TOPOGRAPHY OF ISRAEL**

MEDITERRANEAN
COASTAL PLAIN
JUDEAN HILLS
JORDAN RIVER VALLEY
SYRIAN DESERT

THE ISRAELITES PUSHED THEIR WAY ONTO THE LAND AND SETTLED DOWN. IN TIME, THEY WERE DRAWN TO THE LOCAL CANAANITE GODS.

WE'RE GOING TO A LEWD CEREMONY TO THANK BAAL FOR A GOOD HARVEST.

FOR SHAME! WHAT ABOUT OUR COVENANT?

THE ISRAELITES REMAINED A LOOSE CONFEDERATION OF TRIBES. OVER THEIR TRIBAL CHIEFS, THEY ELECTED **WARRIOR CHIEFS CALLED JUDGES** WHO WERE BELIEVED TO HAVE A DIRECT LINK WITH THE **GOD OF MOSES.**

**FOR 200 YEARS** THESE JUDGES SHOWED UP WHEN NEEDED, INTERPRETING THE LAW AND LEADING THE TRIBES INTO BATTLE. BELOW IS A SELECTION OF THE BETTER KNOWN JUDGES.

**SAMSON,** THE STRONG MAN AND PARTY BOY, LOST HIS HAIR, EYES, AND STRENGTH OVER DELILAH, BUT STILL TOPPLED A PHILISTINE TEMPLE.

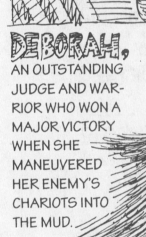

**SAMUEL,** LAST JUDGE, FIRST PROPHET, AND PREMIER POWER BROKER. HE SUPPORTED SAUL AS THE FIRST KING OF THE ISRAELITES. LATER HE REVERSED HIM-SELF AND GAVE THE NOD TO DAVID.

**DEBORAH,** AN OUTSTANDING JUDGE AND WAR-RIOR WHO WON A MAJOR VICTORY WHEN SHE MANEUVERED HER ENEMY'S CHARIOTS INTO THE MUD.

**GIDEON,** THE GREAT GENERAL WHO LOST HIS CHANCE TO BE THE FIRST KING OF THE JEWS BECAUSE HIS SON WAS A MASS MURDERER.

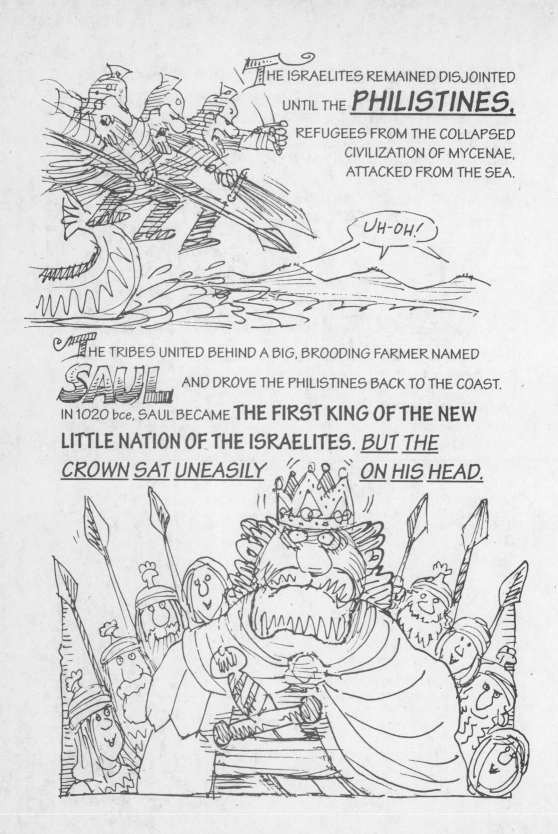

THE ISRAELITES REMAINED DISJOINTED UNTIL THE **PHILISTINES,** REFUGEES FROM THE COLLAPSED CIVILIZATION OF MYCENAE, ATTACKED FROM THE SEA.

UH-OH!

THE TRIBES UNITED BEHIND A BIG, BROODING FARMER NAMED *SAUL* AND DROVE THE PHILISTINES BACK TO THE COAST. IN 1020 bce, SAUL BECAME **THE FIRST KING OF THE NEW LITTLE NATION OF THE ISRAELITES. *BUT THE CROWN SAT UNEASILY ON HIS HEAD.***

UNRELENTING WARFARE FINALLY DROVE SAUL INTO AN EXTREME DEPRESSION.

I NEED CLOSURE!

SAUL GREW JEALOUS AND SUSPICIOUS OF HIS SON-IN-LAW, DAVID. THE CHARISMATIC DAVID WAS FAMOUS FOR HIS POETRY AND FOR HAVING DEFEATED THE PHILISTINE GIANT, GOLIATH, WITH ONLY A SLING.

I WHIRLED IT TWICE AND USED A TWO-FINGER RELEASE.

SAUL HUNTED DAVID, WHO TOOK TO THE HILLS AND BECAME A ROBIN HOOD-LIKE OUTLAW.

WANTED DEAD OR ALIVE DAVID

In 1005 bce, SAUL ENDED UP WITH HIS HEAD DISPLAYED ON A PHILISTINE LANCE.

BOTH THE SOUTHERN ISRAELITE KINGDOM, JUDAH, AND THE NORTHERN, ISRAEL, ELECTED THE POPULAR AND AMBITIOUS DAVID AS THEIR KING. KING DAVID MOVED QUICKLY TO TURN THE YOUNG COUNTRY INTO A MAJOR PLAYER IN THE REGION.

DAVID CONQUERED A JEBUSITE TOWN HIGH IN THE MOUNTAINOUS CENTER OF CANAAN. HE NAMED IT JERUSALEM AND MADE IT HIS CAPITAL.

CLOSE TO GOD AND WITH A GOOD VIEW OF OUR ENEMIES.

THROUGH SHREWD GENERALSHIP AND POLITICAL MANEUVERING, DAVID CREATED AN EMPIRE THAT STRETCHED FROM EGYPT TO THE EUPHRATES. HE INTRODUCED A LUXURIOUS, WORLDLY LIFESTYLE TO THE ISRAELITES.

When King David caught sight of the beautiful Bath-Sheba naked, he arranged her husband's death so he could be with her. But, as an Israelite king, David was judged by the same ethical standards as ordinary people.

FOR SHAME! SINNERS!

NOT FAIR! NO OTHER COUNTRY'S KINGS HAVE TO RUN A GOVERNMENT AND WALK IN THE PATH OF GOD AT THE SAME TIME.

In 970 bce, David, gifted poet, empire builder, sinning king, and spiritual man, lay dying. Beside him were his wife, Bath-Sheba, and their son,

SOLOMON.

DAVID HANDED OVER HIS EMPIRE TO SOLOMON.

WALK IN THE WAY OF GOD, MY SON.

DAD, WE'RE SITTING ON A GOLD MINE. WE CAN COLLECT A TOLL FROM EVERY CARAVAN THAT PASSES BY. LOCATION IS EVERYTHING.

SOLOMON EXPANDED INTERNATIONAL TRADE. WHEN HE MADE A TREATY, HE MARRIED THE DAUGHTER OF THE FOREIGN LEADER. IT WAS SAID HE HAD 999 WIVES.

SOLOMON CREATED A DAZZLING PALACE FOR HIS WIVES **AND A MAGNIFICENT TEMPLE FOR THE ARK OF THE COVENANT.**

THE RIGHT MARRIAGES LEAD TO THE BEST BUSINESS DEALS.

ROYAL WIVES

ROYAL TREASURY

I'M NOT MY FATHER. I HAVE **BIG** IDEAS.

**V**ISITORS ARRIVED FROM ALL OVER TO SEE SOLOMON'S GLAMOROUS KINGDOM AND WORSHIP THE INVISIBLE GOD OF THE ISRAELITES.

## KING SOLOMON WAS SOUGHT

AFTER FOR HIS GREAT WISDOM. HE WAS RENOWNED FOR HIS RIDDLES AND PROVERBS.

GO TO THE ANT, THOU SLUGGARD; CONSIDER HER WAYS, AND BE WISE.

DRINK WATERS OUT OF THINE OWN CISTERN.

THEY SAY HE GETS HIS BEST IDEAS FROM THE BIRDS.

However, the high cost of Solomon's razzle-dazzle expansion divided Israelite society.

About 925 bce, King Solomon died. He'd left his country rich and powerful, and introduced the outside world to the God of Abraham and Moses. But his empire was coming apart.

With Solomon's death, his kingdom split in two: Israel in the north and Judah in the south.

# 3

# THE PORTABLE TORAH

(PROPHETS–SCRIBES)
925 BCE–444 BCE

ISRAEL, THE NORTHERN KINGDOM, WAS MADE UP OF TEN OF THE TWELVE TRIBES OF THE ISRAELITES. FOR TWO HUNDRED YEARS, **ISRAEL WAS AN UNSTABLE LAND WHERE PAGAN GODS MADE A COMEBACK.**

IN THE MIDST OF THIS CHAOS, THERE APPEARED IN ISRAEL A GROUP OF OUTSPOKEN, FEARLESS, REVOLUTIONARY

# PROPHETS

BRINGING WARNINGS FROM GOD AGAINST MORAL BACKSLIDING.

BAAL'S BACK! IT'S TIME FOR WILD PARTIES AND PROFANE SACRIFICES!

IT'S GOOD TO SEE YOUNG PEOPLE EXPRESSING THEMSELVES.

GOD HELP US.

ISRAEL HAS BECOME A BASKET OF ROTTEN FRUIT!

THE PROPHETS—INCLUDING **ELIJAH,** THE SPECTER; **AMOS,** THE WRATHFUL; **HOSEA,** THE GENTLE; AND **ISAIAH,** THE ELOQUENT—THUNDERED AT THE RULING CLASSES FOR THEIR NATIONALISM, PAGANISM, AND OPPRESSION OF THE POOR.

IT IS THE END OF ISRAEL UNLESS YOU RETURN TO BASIC MORAL VALUES.

GOD LOVES YOU EVEN IF YOU HAVE ABANDONED HIM!

IF YOU DON'T LIKE IT HERE, GO TO JUDAH AND PREACH THERE!

AT THE END OF THE 9TH CENTURY bce, A NEW ASIAN EMPIRE, ASSYRIA, OVERPOWERED THE COUNTRIES OF THE MIDDLE EAST. IN 722 bce, SHE EXPELLED THE ISRAELITES FROM THEIR OWN COUNTRY. *THE TEN TRIBES VANISHED AS A PEOPLE AND WERE LOST TO HISTORY.*

STARTING IN 700 bce, ASSYRIA AND OTHER ASIAN POWERS TOOK TURNS OVERRUNNING JUDAH, THEIR GODS AND CULTS TEMPTING THE JEWS. TO BRING THE JEWS BACK TO THEIR GOD, THE PROPHETS AND SCRIBES KICKED OFF A RELIGIOUS REVIVAL.

THIS WAY FOR INTERCOURSE WITH SACRED PRIESTESSES —GUARANTEED TO MAKE YOUR LAND FERTILE.

LEAVE YOUR DEBASED WAYS!

TURN BACK TO THE GOD OF MOSES!

GOD PUNISHES THE IMMORAL!

THEY CENTERED ALL RELIGIOUS CELEBRATIONS IN THE TEMPLE IN JERUSALEM. THEY GATHERED ALL THE OLD TEXTS AND CODES OF THE JEWS, AND REINTRODUCED THEM IN AN EASY-TO-UNDERSTAND WAY AS HUMANE PRINCIPLES, ETHICS, AND RITUALS TO LIVE BY.

CANCEL DEBTS EVERY SEVEN YEARS.

PROTECT THE POOR.

DO NOT MUZZLE THE OX AS IT TREADS THE CORN.

HEN, IN 622 bce, KING JOSIAH, WHILE REPAIRING THE TEMPLE, DISCOVERED AN ANCIENT PARCHMENT ON WHICH WAS WRITTEN THE SACRED LAW OF MOSES. _AGAIN, THE JEWS WOULD FIND THEIR WAY TO GOD THROUGH THE WRITTEN WORD._

THIS SCROLL CONTAINS THE WORDS OF GOD AS WRITTEN DOWN BY MOSES HIMSELF.

YOU THINK WE WERE BORN YESTERDAY? YOU PLANTED IT THERE.

WHATEVER. BUT IT MEANS THAT WE MUST REDEDICATE OURSELVES TO GOD!

HE PROPHET JEREMIAH SHOWED UP AT THIS TIME. HE PROMOTED THE IDEA THAT THE GOD OF THE JEWS WAS NOT A NATIONAL GOD BUT A UNIVERSAL GOD.

HE IS THE GOD OF EVERY INDIVIDUAL ON EARTH.

I STILL CAN'T SEE HIM.

BUT, YOU CAN READ WHAT HE SAYS.

43

# BABYLON

By the sixth century bce, BABYLON, LED BY THE GREAT **NEBUCHADNEZZAR**, DEFEATED ASSYRIA AND INHERITED JUDAH. LITTLE JUDAH STOOD UP TO MIGHTY BABYLON. JEREMIAH PUSHED PACIFISM.

RESISTANCE IS NATIONAL SUICIDE!

Jewish militants called Jeremiah a traitor and threw him down a well. Jeremiah displayed a trait that Jews would carry through history: **FINDING SIGNIFICANCE IN EVERYTHING.**

IF WE LOSE, IT'LL BE GOD'S WAY OF TEACHING US TO OVERCOME ADVERSITY.

**I**N 586 bce, NEBUCHADNEZZAR BROKE JEWISH RESISTANCE. HE PLUNDERED JERUSALEM AND **DESTROYED THE TEMPLE.**

**I**T WAS AT THIS TIME THAT THE ARK OF THE COVENANT DISAPPEARED FROM HISTORY.

**T**O WEAKEN RESISTANCE, NEBUCHADNEZZAR TRANSPORTED ALL THE INFLUENTIAL JEWS BACK TO HIS CAPITAL, **BABYLON.**

**S**OME JEWS CONTINUED TO FIGHT AMONG THE RUINS. OTHERS ESCAPED TO EGYPT, TAKING JEREMIAH WITH THEM.

WE ARE DISPERSED BECAUSE GOD WANTS US TO FEEL DESPAIR!

ENOUGH, ALREADY. IT'S OVER.

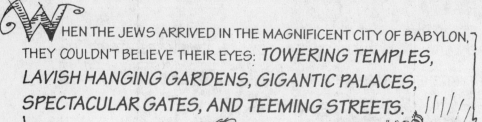

WHEN THE JEWS ARRIVED IN THE MAGNIFICENT CITY OF BABYLON, THEY COULDN'T BELIEVE THEIR EYES: *TOWERING TEMPLES, LAVISH HANGING GARDENS, GIGANTIC PALACES, SPECTACULAR GATES, AND TEEMING STREETS.*

IN BABYLON, SOME JEWS ADJUSTED EASILY. OTHERS WERE NOSTALGIC.

REMEMBER, GOD TRAVELS. HE IS HERE IN BABYLON WITH YOU.

INSPIRED BY THE PROPHET EZEKIEL, THE JEWS OF BABYLON CAME UP WITH THE IDEA FOR THE

# SYNAGOGUE

— A COMMUNAL PLACE TO MEET AND PRAY, LED BY LAY TEACHERS (THE FIRST RABBIS).

I HAVE SOMETHING TO SAY ABOUT THE SABBATH.

YOU ALWAYS HAVE SOMETHING TO SAY ABOUT THE SABBATH.

I DISAGREE WITH WHATEVER YOU HAVE TO SAY.

I DON'T FEEL LONELY ANYMORE.

I THINK I HEAR SOMETHING.

IN 539 bce, **CYRUS**, BRILLIANT LEADER OF A NEW EASTERN KINGDOM, PERSIA, TOPPLED BABYLON. THE PROPHETS TRIED TO MAKE SENSE OF THOSE CHAOTIC TIMES.

GRASS WITHERS, FLOWERS FADE, GOD STANDS FOREVER.

AMAZINGLY, CYRUS PROVED TO BE A DIFFERENT KIND OF LEADER. HE SAID THE JEWS OF BABYLON COULD GO HOME IF THEY WANTED.

SO, LET'S GO.

BACK TO THAT PILE OF ROCKS? NO WAY. WE HAVE OUR FAMILY AND BUSINESS HERE.

YOU GO. WE'LL RAISE MONEY IN SYNAGOGUE TO PAY YOUR WAY.

THE JEWS BUILT A SMALL TEMPLE IN JERUSALEM, BUT TIMES REMAINED HARD UNTIL **NEHEMIAH,** A POLITICIAN, AND **EZRA,** A SCRIBE, _LED A REBIRTH OF JEWISH CONFIDENCE AND FAITH._

EZRA SAID WE SHOULD STOP MARRYING NON-JEWISH WOMEN.

OH? AND WHERE DOES HE THINK OUR CHILDREN'S NICE LONG LEGS CAME FROM? NOT YOUR SIDE.

EZRA GATHERED AND COMPILED ALL THE OLD TEXTS OF THE SACRED LAW OF MOSES. TOGETHER THEY BECAME THE

TORAH, MADE UP

OF THE BOOKS OF *GENESIS, EXODUS, LEVITICUS, NUMBERS,* AND *DEUTERONOMY.*

YOU CAN LOOK IT UP. IT'S ALL HERE: THE WILL OF GOD, THE MEANING OF LIFE, THE ROLE OF THE JEWS IN HISTORY...

...PLUS LOTS OF CELEBRITY GOSSIP, AND GREAT STORIES OF CRIME, SEX, POLITICS, AND RETRIBUTION.

IN 444 bce, EZRA ASSEMBLED JEWS FROM FAR AND WIDE IN JERUSALEM AND READ TO THEM FROM THE TORAH. *AND WITH THAT READING, THE JEWISH PEOPLE WERE ONCE AGAIN INSPIRED TO RECOGNIZE THE TORAH AS THE BASIS OF JUDAISM AND THEIR DIVINE LINK WITH GOD.*

OF COURSE, THE JEWS WERE FREE TO DO WHAT THEY'D ALWAYS DONE: DEBATE, DISAGREE, ARGUE, NEGOTIATE.

AT THIS TIME, SOME JEWS BEGAN TO MOVE BEYOND THEIR HOMELAND IN SEARCH OF OPPORTUNITY AND ADVENTURE. AND WITH THEM WENT THEIR PORTABLE TORAH.

BACK IN JUDAH, THE HIGH PRIESTS STILL FOCUSED ALL RELIGIOUS ACTIVITY IN THE CENTRAL TEMPLE.

BUT ALL THE JEWS OF THE REGION WERE ABOUT TO MEET A POWER GREATER THAN ANY THEY'D MET SO FAR. OUT OF THE WEST CAME THE GREEKS.

UH, OH!

THE GREEKS DIDN'T EVEN KNOW ABOUT THE JEWISH NATION. THEY'D NAMED THE AREA AROUND JERUSALEM PALESTINE AFTER THE PHILISTINES.

# 4

# THE WEST, READY OR NOT

### (GREEKS-ROMANS)
332 BCE–135 CE

# THE GREEKS

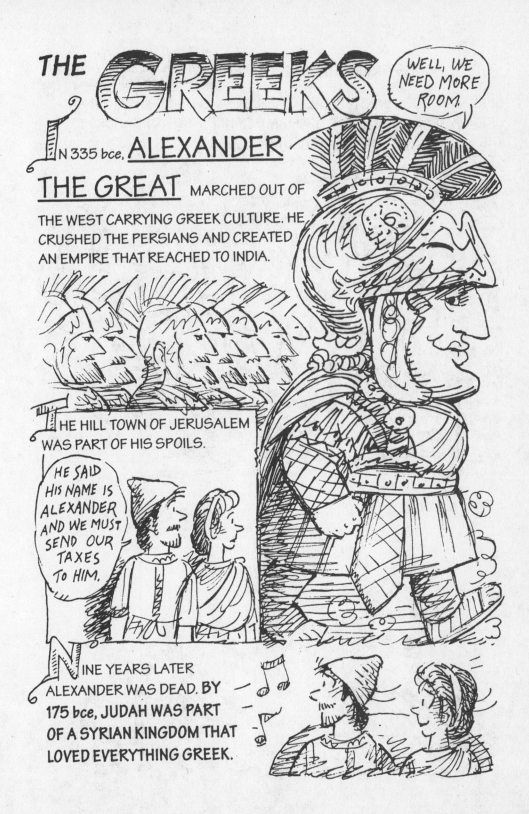

"WELL, WE NEED MORE ROOM."

IN 335 bce, **ALEXANDER THE GREAT** MARCHED OUT OF THE WEST CARRYING GREEK CULTURE. HE CRUSHED THE PERSIANS AND CREATED AN EMPIRE THAT REACHED TO INDIA.

THE HILL TOWN OF JERUSALEM WAS PART OF HIS SPOILS.

"HE SAID HIS NAME IS ALEXANDER AND WE MUST SEND OUR TAXES TO HIM."

NINE YEARS LATER ALEXANDER WAS DEAD. BY 175 bce, JUDAH WAS PART OF A SYRIAN KINGDOM THAT LOVED EVERYTHING GREEK.

THE GLORIOUS GREEK CULTURE, CALLED **HELLENISM,** SPREAD ACROSS WESTERN ASIA. HELLENISM'S SOPHISTICATION AND ORIGINALITY IN PHILOSOPHY, DRAMA, SCIENCE, AND ART SHOOK UP THE SLEEPY EAST AND, IN PARTICULAR ▫ ▫ ▫

**...THE JEWS,** SOME OF WHOM HAD MOVED WEST, SETTLING IN HELLENISTIC TOWNS AROUND THE MEDITERRANEAN.

IN TIME, JEWS LIVING IN HELLENISTIC TOWNS FORGOT THEIR HEBREW. IN **ALEXANDRIA, EGYPT,** THEY TRANSLATED THE TORAH INTO GREEK. THIS ALSO HELPED INTRODUCE THEIR GOD TO THE GREEK WORLD.

THE JEWS IN THEIR NEW COMMUNITIES FOUND THAT THERE WERE _BUSINESS AND CULTURAL ADVANTAGES_ TO INCLUDING HELLENISM IN THEIR LIVES.

Y'SEE, HE'S INVISIBLE BUT UNIVERSAL.

UH, HUH. ???

SO INSTEAD OF CALLING IT GOD'S COVENANT, WE'LL SAY IT'S ABRAHAM'S EXCLUSIVE MEMBERSHIP IN GOD'S GYMNASIUM.

CLUB MEMBERS ONLY
HOURS / RATES

**INSIDE** JUDAH, HELLENISM CREATED CONFLICT. JUDAISM WAS ABOUT MORAL ABSOLUTES. THE GREEKS BELIEVED IN **SELF-EXPRESSION, SKEPTICISM,** AND **PLEASURE.**

JEWISH SOCIETY REACTED TO THESE GREEK INFLUENCES BY SPLITTING INTO OPPOSING POLITICAL CAMPS.

THE SYRIAN KING TRIED TO UNIFY AND STRENGTHEN HIS EMPIRE BY **FORCING MORE GREEK CULTURE** ON HIS SUBJECTS.

IN THE TEMPLE IN JERUSALEM, THE KING INSTALLED STATUES OF A GREEK/EGYPTIAN/JEWISH GOD.

ONE SIZE FITS ALL. VERY EFFICIENT.

HORRIFIED, MODERATES AND PIETISTS PROPELLED HELLENISTS AND STATUES FROM THE TEMPLE WALLS.

YOWWW

THE KING STRUCK BACK BY OUTLAWING JEWISH OBSERVANCE.

IN RETALIATION, AN OLD PRIEST, **MATTATHIAS HASMON,** KILLED A JEW MAKING A SACRIFICE TO A GREEK GOD. *THEN HE AND HIS FIVE SONS TOOK TO THE HILLS.*

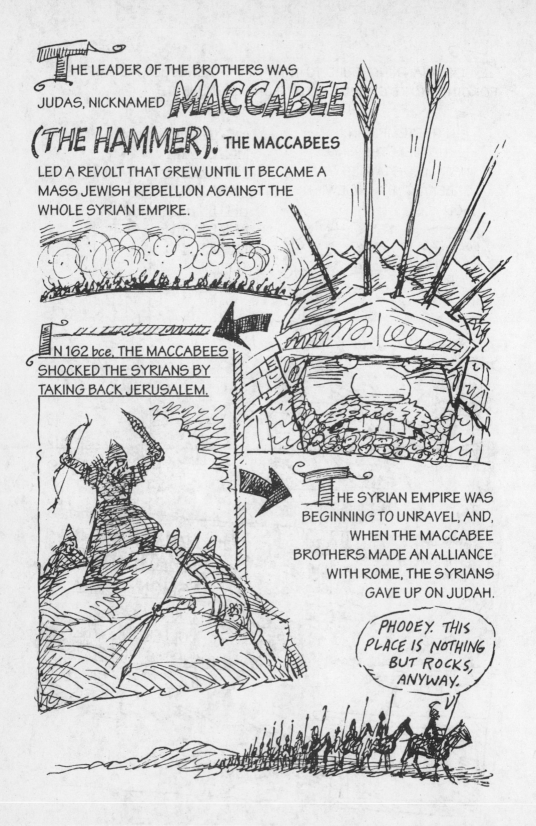

THE LEADER OF THE BROTHERS WAS JUDAS, NICKNAMED **MACCABEE (THE HAMMER).** THE MACCABEES LED A REVOLT THAT GREW UNTIL IT BECAME A MASS JEWISH REBELLION AGAINST THE WHOLE SYRIAN EMPIRE.

IN 162 bce, THE MACCABEES SHOCKED THE SYRIANS BY TAKING BACK JERUSALEM.

THE SYRIAN EMPIRE WAS BEGINNING TO UNRAVEL, AND, WHEN THE MACCABEE BROTHERS MADE AN ALLIANCE WITH ROME, THE SYRIANS GAVE UP ON JUDAH.

PHOOEY. THIS PLACE IS NOTHING BUT ROCKS, ANYWAY.

**ONCE MORE, THE JEWS WERE IN CHARGE OF THEIR OWN COUNTRY,** BUT NOT FOR LONG. THE HASMONAEAN RULERS, FROM THE PIOUS MACCABEE LINE, TURNED OUT TO BE PETTY TYRANTS.

YOU TRY TO RUN A MODERN COUNTRY AND A RELIGION AT THE SAME TIME. ALL YOU DO IS MAKE ENEMIES.

**THREE SECTS** FORMED IN RESPONSE TO HASMONAEAN POLICIES.

THE **PHARISEES** HAD A LIBERAL VIEW OF THE BIBLE BUT WERE AGAINST GREEK INFLUENCES.

MY DAUGHTER IS NOT GOING OUT IN GREEK FASHIONS.

BUT IT'S SO COOL, DAD.

THE **SADDUCEES** SUPPORTED A LITERAL VIEW OF THE BIBLE AND GREEK POWER AND INFLUENCE.

WE BELIEVE IN THE PRIEST-HOOD...

...AND TRICKLE-DOWN ECONOMICS.

THE **ESSENES** WERE RELIGIOUS PURISTS WHO LIVED MONASTIC LIVES.

LATER, THE **ZEALOTS**, POLITICAL EXTREMISTS, WOULD LEAD THE REBELLION AGAINST ROME.

THE LAST HASMONAEAN MONARCH WAS AN ENLIGHTENED WOMAN, **QUEEN ALEXANDRA.** HER REIGN WAS A GOLDEN AGE OF THE JEWS.

WOMAN'S WORK IS NEVER DONE.

WHEN ALEXANDRA DIED, HER TWO SONS FOUGHT OVER HER CROWN. EACH BROTHER PLEADED WITH MIGHTY **ROME** FOR HELP.

BUT ROME HELPED HERSELF.

# THE ROMANS

I THINK BIG!

IN 67 bce, ROME GRABBED JUDAH FOR HERSELF. SHE RENAMED IT JUDEA AND MADE IT PART OF **THE GREAT ROMAN EMPIRE.** IN 37 bce, SHE APPOINTED A LOCAL POLITICO, <u>HEROD,</u> KING OF THE JEWS.

**HEROD** BUILT BIG, TAXED BIG, AND PUSHED EVERYTHING GREEK. HE CONSTRUCTED A COUNTRY FORTRESS FOR HIMSELF ON A HUGE ROCK CALLED <u>*MASADA*</u> NEAR THE DEAD SEA . *HE EXPANDED* THE <u>TEMPLE</u> *TILL IT WAS LARGER THAN SOLOMON'S.*

63

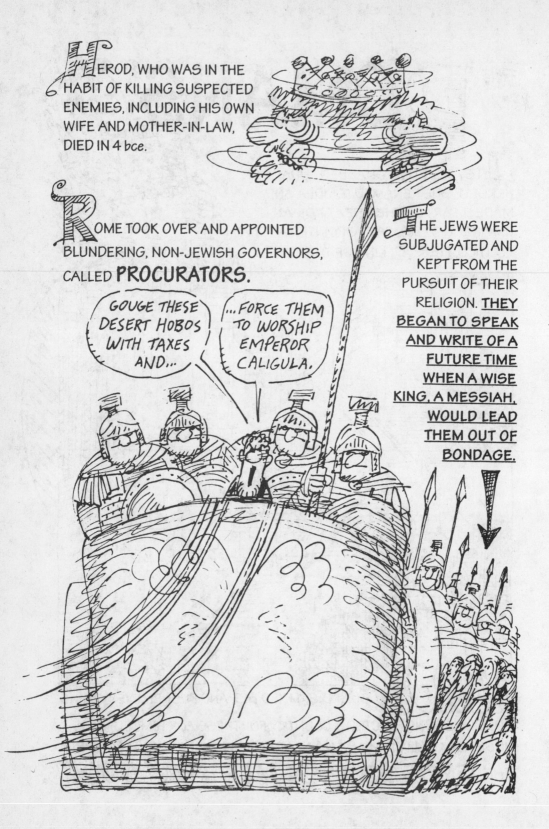

**H**EROD, WHO WAS IN THE HABIT OF KILLING SUSPECTED ENEMIES, INCLUDING HIS OWN WIFE AND MOTHER-IN-LAW, DIED IN 4 bce.

**R**OME TOOK OVER AND APPOINTED BLUNDERING, NON-JEWISH GOVERNORS, CALLED **PROCURATORS.**

GOUGE THESE DESERT HOBOS WITH TAXES AND...

...FORCE THEM TO WORSHIP EMPEROR CALIGULA.

**T**HE JEWS WERE SUBJUGATED AND KEPT FROM THE PURSUIT OF THEIR RELIGION. THEY BEGAN TO SPEAK AND WRITE OF A FUTURE TIME WHEN A WISE KING, A MESSIAH, WOULD LEAD THEM OUT OF BONDAGE.

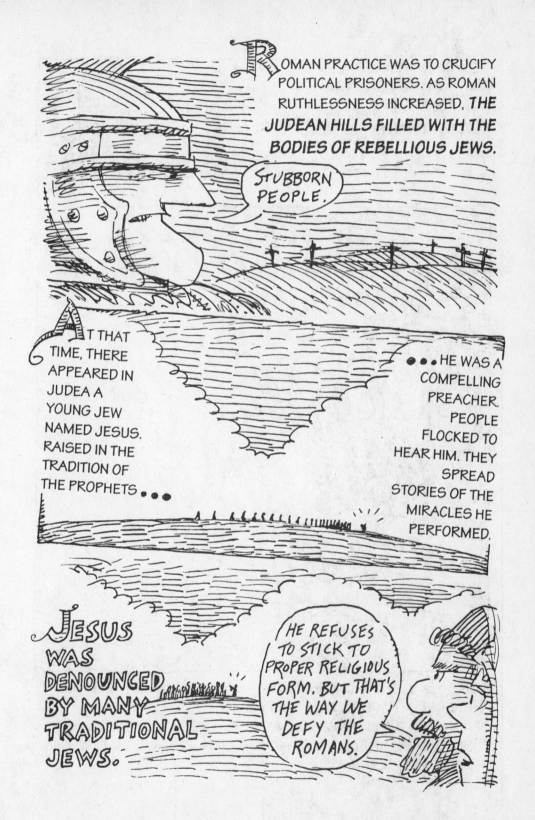

ESUS WORRIED THE ROMANS WHO VIEWED HIM AS A **POLITICAL REVOLUTIONARY.**

N 33 *ce*, JESUS AND HIS FOLLOWERS WERE IN JERUSALEM FOR THE FEAST OF PASSOVER. JESUS PREACHED HUMILITY AND DENOUNCED THE EXTRAVAGANT ATMOSPHERE OF THE TEMPLE. HE PUSHED OVER THE BOOTHS OF MONEY CHANGERS AND SELLERS OF SACRIFICIAL PIGEONS.

**P**HARISEES AND SADDUCEES ACCUSED JESUS OF BEING A TROUBLE-MAKER. THE ROMAN GOVERNOR, PONTIUS PILATE, DECLARED JESUS A DANGEROUS EXTREMIST AND HAD HIM CRUCIFIED.

**T**HREE DAYS LATER, JESUS' FOLLOWERS SAW HIM RISE FROM THE DEAD. THE EVENT CAUSED LITTLE NOTICE AT A TIME WHEN SO MANY JEWS WERE BEING CRUCIFIED.

**T**HE LAST PROCURATOR WAS SO CRUEL AND CORRUPT THAT *JUDEA FINALLY ROSE UP IN REBELLION.*

**L**ED BY THE ZEALOTS, JEWISH FIGHTERS CAPTURED THE **MOUNTAIN FORTRESS OF MASADA.**

IN 66 ce, THE JEWS DROVE THE SUPPOSEDLY INVINCIBLE ROMANS OUT OF JERUSALEM **AND TOOK BACK THEIR COUNTRY.**

In **70 ce**, AGAINST TENACIOUS JEWISH RESISTANCE, ELITE ROMAN LEGIONS, WITH THEIR HUGE BATTERING RAMS, REGAINED JERUSALEM *AND DESTROYED THE TEMPLE.*

✻ SEE P. 71

**M**ASADA HELD OUT FOR THREE YEARS. WHEN THE ROMANS REACHED THE SUMMIT, THEY FOUND THAT THE REMAINING DEFENDERS HAD KILLED EACH OTHER RATHER THAN SURRENDER THEIR FREEDOM.

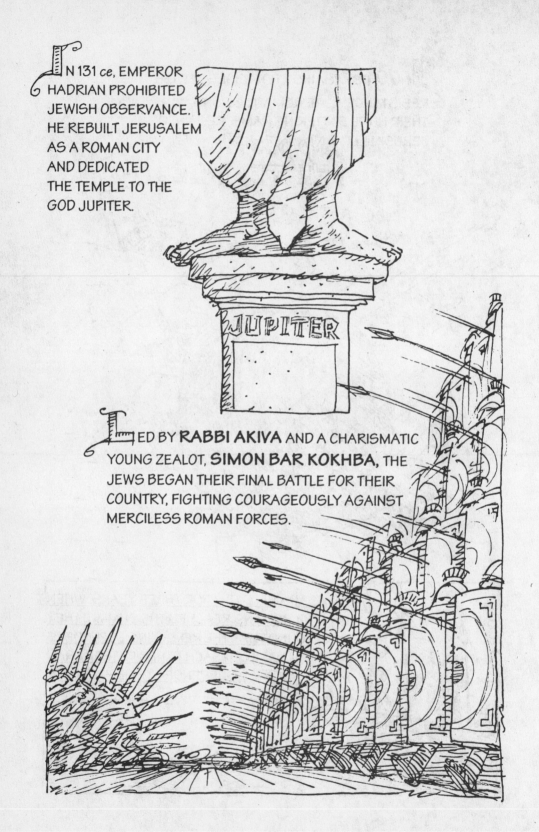

IN 131 ce, EMPEROR HADRIAN PROHIBITED JEWISH OBSERVANCE. HE REBUILT JERUSALEM AS A ROMAN CITY AND DEDICATED THE TEMPLE TO THE GOD JUPITER.

JUPITER

LED BY **RABBI AKIVA** AND A CHARISMATIC YOUNG ZEALOT, **SIMON BAR KOKHBA,** THE JEWS BEGAN THEIR FINAL BATTLE FOR THEIR COUNTRY, FIGHTING COURAGEOUSLY AGAINST MERCILESS ROMAN FORCES.

ROMAN POWER GROUND THE JEWS DOWN. BY 135 ce,
JUDEA WAS GONE. IT WAS RENAMED <u>SYRIA PALESTINA</u>.
JEWISH PRISONERS WERE TAKEN TO THE SLAVE MARKETS
OF ROME (WHERE THEY WOULD BE AMONG THE EARLIEST
ANCESTORS OF EUROPEAN JEWRY).

✱ FROM P. 69

DURING THE SIEGE OF JERUSALEM, THE ZEALOTS
WOULDN'T LET ANYONE LEAVE THE CITY. BUT JOHANAN BEN
ZAKKAI, A SCHOLAR DRIVEN TO MAKE SURE JUDAISM WOULD
SURVIVE, HID HIMSELF IN A COFFIN AND WAS CARRIED OUT.

MAKE WAY! DEAD BODY!
PLAGUE VICTIM. DON'T
GET TOO CLOSE.

OOF. TAKE IT
EASY, GUYS!

THE WORLD OF THE TEMPLE AND THE PRIESTHOOD WAS GONE. BEN ZAKKAI WENT ON TO FOUND ACADEMIES OF JEWISH LEARNING. **THE TOUGH JEWISH FIGHTERS PUT ASIDE THEIR WEAPONS AND BECAME STUDENTS, THE KEEPERS OF JEWISH CULTURE.**

# II

# THE PEOPLE FROM SOMEWHERE ELSE

# 5

## PLAYING BY THE RULES

### (TALMUD–CHRISTIANS)
### 70 CE–500 CE

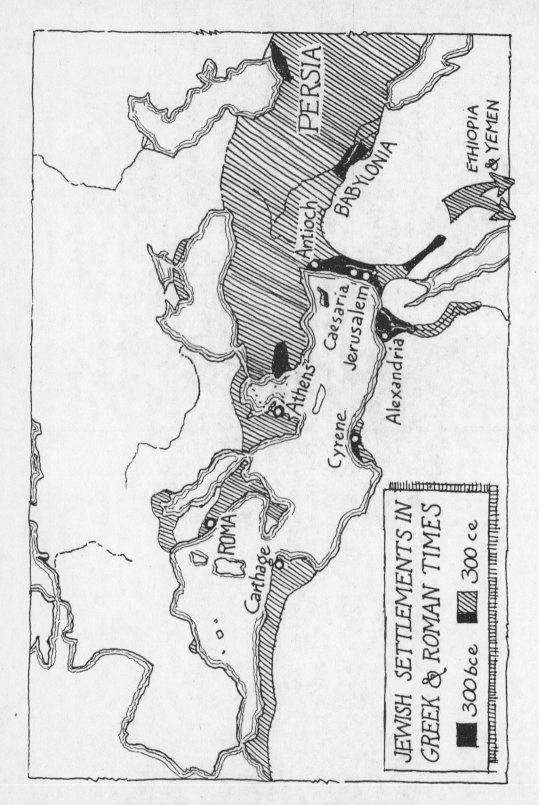

PERSIA

BABYLONIA

ETHIOPIA & YEMEN

Antioch

Caesaria
Jerusalem

Athens

Cyrene

Alexandria

ROMA
Carthage

JEWISH SETTLEMENTS IN
GREEK & ROMAN TIMES

300 bce
300 ce

THE JEWS, NOW LANDLESS VAGABONDS, **HIT THE ROAD,** JOINING OTHER JEWS WHO'D LEFT JUDEA IN EARLIER TIMES. TOGETHER THEY FORMED THE

DIASPORA

UNLIKE OTHER NATIONS FROM THE DISTANT PAST, THEY WEREN'T ABOUT TO LET THEIR CULTURE SURVIVE ONLY AS A FOOTNOTE IN A HISTORY BOOK.

MORE THAN ENOUGH!

WHAT'S THE DIASPORA?

IT'S WHEN WE LEAVE OUR ANCESTRAL HOMELAND, SCATTER AROUND THE WORLD, YET REMAIN JEWS.

I ALREADY MISS OUR COUNTRY.

BUT WE HAVE OUR TORAH.

IT'LL BE UP TO US RABBIS TO MAKE SURE THE JEWS OF THE DIASPORA STAY TRUE TO JEWISH LAW.

BEN ZAKKAI'S DISCIPLES SET UP YESHIVAS IN NORTHERN PALESTINE.

THESE SCHOLARS BEGAN TO SORT THROUGH ALL THE RICH HISTORICAL BOOKS OF THE JEWS. THOSE WORDS THEY FELT WERE INSPIRED BY GOD, THEY DECLARED SACRED.

THIS IS SACRED. IT STAYS IN!

NOT SACRED. OUT!

JUDAISM IS ABOUT LIFE ON EARTH. THIS IS ABOUT HEAVEN. MAYBE THE CHRISTIANS CAN USE IT. OUT!

WHEN THEY FINISHED, THEY ANNOUNCED THE COMPLETED HEBREW BIBLE, MADE UP OF *THE* *TORAH,* THE WORDS OF *THE* *PROPHETS,* AND *THE* *WRITINGS.*

תורה נביאים כתובים

**BUT,** IT WAS NOT ALWAYS CLEAR HOW TO APPLY GOD'S WORDS TO DAILY LIFE. SINCE THE DAYS OF EZRA, PUNDITS HAD BEEN INTERPRETING THE SACRED TEXT.

MY FATHER WON'T LET ME MARRY JACOB. WHAT SHOULD I DO?

MY REAL ESTATE DEAL IS GOING SOUR. CAN THE TORAH HELP?

I WILL ILLUSTRATE GOD'S WISDOM WITH A STORY.

AROUND 200 ce, THE RABBIS GATHERED TOGETHER THIS VAST BODY OF ORAL LAW AND TRADITION. **THEY STUDIED THE PROBLEM-SOLVING TECHNIQUES AND INTERPRETATIONS OF THE PUNDITS.**

DISCUSSIONS OF WIT AND WISDOM OVER THERE.

RULES AND REGULATIONS HERE.

ANALYSIS AND DEBATE INSIDE.

WHAT DO WE DO ABOUT GREEK SKEPTICISM?

THROW IT OUT!

NO! LEAVE IT IN!

THEY ANALYZED EVERY **WORD AND INFLECTION**, EVERY **EXCLAMATION POINT, COMMA, AND PERIOD,** SEARCHING FOR MEANINGS.

SOB!

HA, HA, HA!

JEWISH SCRIBES LEARNED EARLY THE VALUE OF ENTERTAINMENT IN HOLDING PEOPLE'S ATTENTION.

IF IT'S A COMMA, GOD PROVES MY POINT.

IF IT'S A PERIOD, HE PROVES MINE.

I THINK IT'S A GREASE SPOT.

IF IT'S A GREASE SPOT, WE MUST START THE DEBATE ALL OVER AGAIN.

LED BY JUDAH THE PRINCE, THE SCHOLARS CATEGORIZED AND GROUPED THE BEST OF THE ORAL TEACHINGS AND INTERPRETATIONS, INSIGHTS AND ETHICS, REGULATIONS AND RULES, AND _WOVE THEM TOGETHER INTO A TEXT._

THIS IS ABOUT SHEEP. WE DON'T KEEP SHEEP.

THIS IS ABOUT TEMPLE SACRIFICE. THERE'S NO MORE TEMPLE.

DOESN'T MATTER, JUST MEMORIZE IT.

THEY CALLED THIS BODY OF WISDOM BASED ON THE TORAH THE **MISHNAH**, *MEANING TO REVIEW.* SOME RABBIS WORRIED THAT A WRITTEN MISHNAH WOULD COMPETE WITH THE TORAH.

IT MUST REMAIN IN ORAL FORM ONLY.

THAT'S A LOT TO MEMORIZE.

THE MISHNAH WAS FINALLY CODIFIED. BUT JEWISH LEADERSHIP WAS SHIFTING FROM PALESTINE TO BABYLONIA.

THE MISHNAH IS CLOSED, BUT WE HAVE MUCH MORE TO SAY.

I'M GETTING...

... A HEADACHE.

A RENOWNED SCHOLAR OF THE TIME WAS A WOMAN, **BERURIAH.** BERURIAH WAS ALSO KNOWN FOR HER BITING WIT, ESPECIALLY WHEN IT CAME TO DEFLECTING FOOLISH QUESTIONS FROM MEN.

DON'T YOU KNOW THAT WOMEN ARE TOO SHALLOW FOR YOUR QUESTIONS?

IN PALESTINE AND THEN IN BABYLONIA, DISCUSSIONS, STORIES, AND ELABORATIONS ACCUMULATED ABOUT THE MISHNAH. THEY WERE CALLED THE **GEMARAH,** THE SUPPLEMENT.

OY!

THERE ARE THOUSANDS OF LINES OF GEMARAH FOR EVERY LINE OF MISHNAH.

THE MISHNAH AND THE GEMARAH TOGETHER MADE UP THE

**TALMUD.** THE STUDY OF THE TALMUD WOULD LIGHT THE WAY FOR THE JEWISH PEOPLE THROUGH THE CENTURIES...

...AND SHARPEN THE SKILLS OF FUTURE LAWYERS, SONG WRITERS, TALK-SHOW HOSTS, STAND-UP COMICS, AND KIBBITZERS.

HAVE YOU HEARD THE ONE ABOUT THE RABBI WHO...

OH, I KNOW THAT ONE. IT'S NOT FUNNY.

BECAUSE YOU DON'T TELL IT RIGHT. I'LL TELL IT.

THIS VAST QUANTITY OF JEWISH KNOWLEDGE WAS CARRIED FROM ACADEMY TO ACADEMY BY STUDENTS HONORED FOR THEIR EXTRAORDINARY MEMORIES.

AT THE SAME TIME, RELIGIOUS PERSECUTIONS, CHANGES OF RULERS, AND INVADERS FROM ASIA BROUGHT UNCERTAINTY AND BLOODY TROUBLE TO EASTERN JEWISH COMMUNITIES, AND DANGER TO HEADS FULL OF **MISHNAH** AND **GEMARAH**.

THIS IS NOT GOOD. BETTER TO WRITE IT DOWN THAN TO LOSE IT.

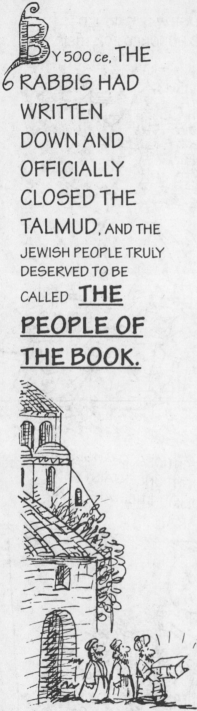

BY 500 ce, THE RABBIS HAD WRITTEN DOWN AND OFFICIALLY CLOSED THE TALMUD, AND THE JEWISH PEOPLE TRULY DESERVED TO BE CALLED **THE PEOPLE OF THE BOOK.**

THEY HAVE A LOT TO SAY ABOUT WHAT I HAD TO SAY.

NOW WE BACK UP TO THE EARLY YEARS OF THE COMMON ERA AND THE LARGE JEWISH COMMUNITY LIVING IN

# ROME.

THE JEWS HAD IT OKAY. WHAT'S ONE MORE GOD IN A TOWN FULL OF GODS?

AROUND 60 ce, AN ODD, EDUCATED JEW NAMED **PAUL** BECAME CHIEF PRESS AGENT FOR A MINOR JEWISH SECT CALLED **CHRISTIANS.** PAUL BEGAN PREACHING THAT JEWISH LAW WASN'T BINDING.

FORGET FINDING GOD THROUGH A BOOK!

FORGET THE BOOK?!?

PAUL BROKE WITH THE JEWS AND TOOK HIS MESSAGE DIRECTLY TO THE PAGANS.

MONOTHEISM MADE EASY. GAIN WITHOUT PAIN!

...FORGET DIETARY RULES, CIRCUMCISION, AND THE SABBATH. JUST ACCEPT JESUS CHRIST AND FIND REDEMPTION.

OUTSIDE INVADERS AND INTERNAL CORRUPTION SAPPED ROME'S STRENGTH. DESPERATE FOR STABILITY, PEOPLE EVEN CREATED NEW GODS.

I DON'T THINK IT WORKS.

IN 313 ce, EMPEROR CONSTANTINE CAME UP WITH A PLAN TO UNIFY HIS SHAKY EMPIRE.

THE LARGEST AND ANGRIEST GROUP IN ROME ARE POOR. THE CHRISTIANS APPEAL TO THE POOR. THEREFORE...

SALVATION THROUGH JESUS

CHRISTIANITY, OFFICIAL RELIGION OF THE ROMAN EMPIRE
Constantine

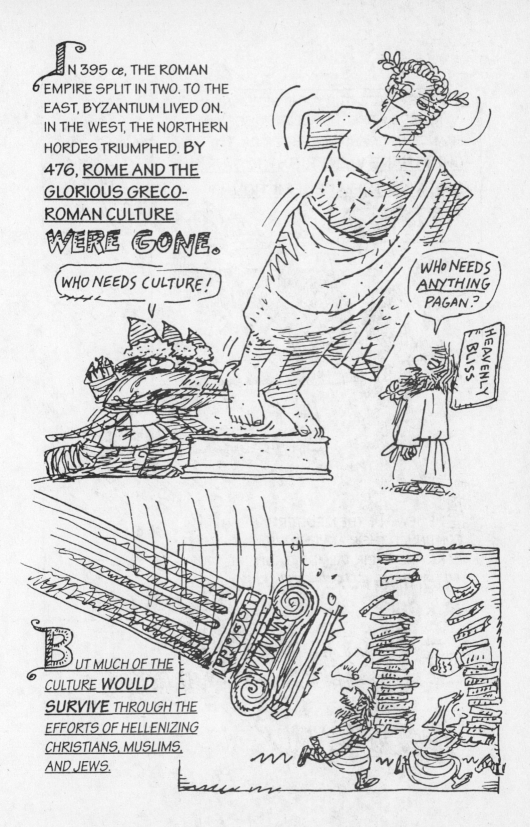

IN 395 CE, THE ROMAN EMPIRE SPLIT IN TWO. TO THE EAST, BYZANTIUM LIVED ON. IN THE WEST, THE NORTHERN HORDES TRIUMPHED. BY 476, <u>ROME AND THE GLORIOUS GRECO-ROMAN CULTURE</u> WERE GONE.

WHO NEEDS CULTURE!

WHO NEEDS ANYTHING PAGAN?

HEAVENLY BLISS

BUT MUCH OF THE CULTURE **WOULD SURVIVE** THROUGH THE EFFORTS OF HELLENIZING CHRISTIANS, MUSLIMS, AND JEWS.

BY THE 6TH CENTURY, THE GERMANIC WARLORDS WERE THE RULERS OF SPAIN, FRANCE, ITALY, AND NORTH AFRICA. **THE CHRISTIANS WENT RIGHT TO WORK OFFERING THEM REDEMPTION.**

CHECK IT OUT!

DIVINE MERCY

THE JEWS OF THE MEDITERRANEAN CONTINUED THEIR ADVENTURE, CARRYING THEIR TALMUDIC CULTURE, *PUSHING FURTHER INTO EUROPE.*

WHERE TO?

WHERE THERE IS FREEDOM AND OPPORTUNITY.

# 6

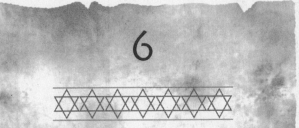

# THE
# ADAPTABLE
# PEOPLE

(ISLAM–FEUDALISM)
500 CE–1000 CE

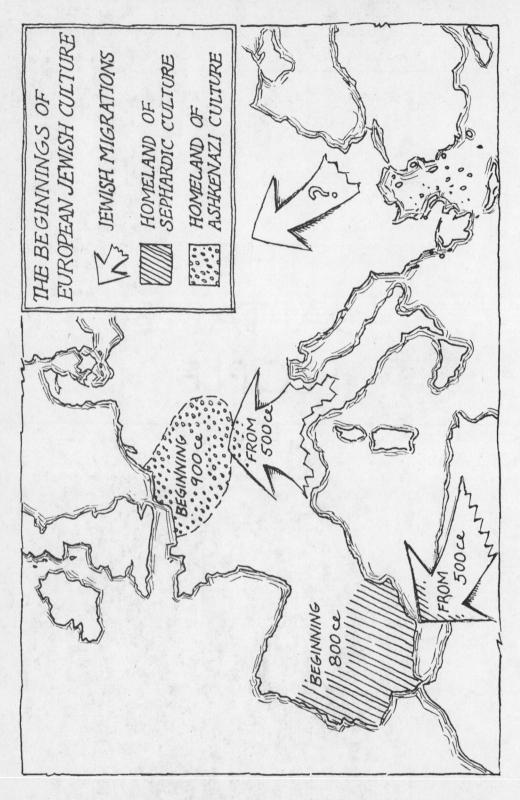

THE BEGINNINGS OF
EUROPEAN JEWISH CULTURE

JEWISH MIGRATIONS

HOMELAND OF
SEPHARDIC CULTURE

HOMELAND OF
ASHKENAZI CULTURE

?

FROM
500 ce

FROM
500 ce

BEGINNING
900 ce

BEGINNING
800 ce

# ISLAM

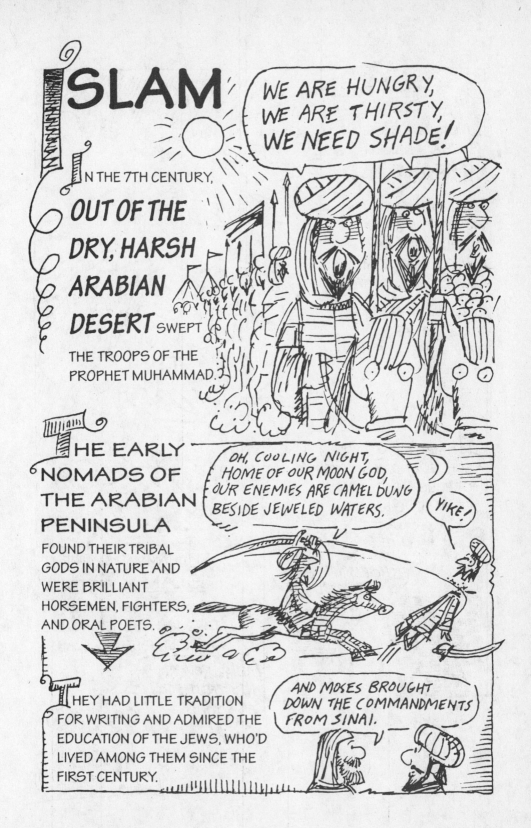

IN THE 7TH CENTURY, **OUT OF THE DRY, HARSH ARABIAN DESERT** SWEPT THE TROOPS OF THE PROPHET MUHAMMAD.

WE ARE HUNGRY, WE ARE THIRSTY, WE NEED SHADE!

**THE EARLY NOMADS OF THE ARABIAN PENINSULA** FOUND THEIR TRIBAL GODS IN NATURE AND WERE BRILLIANT HORSEMEN, FIGHTERS, AND ORAL POETS.

OH, COOLING NIGHT, HOME OF OUR MOON GOD, OUR ENEMIES ARE CAMEL DUNG BESIDE JEWELED WATERS.

YIKE!

**THEY HAD LITTLE TRADITION** FOR WRITING AND ADMIRED THE EDUCATION OF THE JEWS, WHO'D LIVED AMONG THEM SINCE THE FIRST CENTURY.

AND MOSES BROUGHT DOWN THE COMMANDMENTS FROM SINAI.

IN 610 ce, A CAMEL MERCHANT NAMED **MUHAMMAD** RECEIVED A DIVINE MESSAGE IN A CAVE OUTSIDE THE OASIS TOWN OF MECCA. AN ANGEL TOLD HIM THAT **ALLAH** (GOD) WAS ONE AND THAT MUHAMMAD WAS HIS MESSENGER.

IN MANY WAYS, ISLAM ECHOED JUDAISM. BUT, NOT GETTING ANY SUPPORT FROM JEWS ...

HEY, OUR GOD HAS ALREADY SHOWN UP. CASE CLOSED.

...MUHAMMAD CLAIMED **ISLAM** AS THE TRUE FAITH AND UNIFIED ARABIA THROUGH A BELIEF IN THE UNIQUENESS OF ALLAH.

ALLAH REVEALED HIS TRUTH TO ABRAHAM AND MUHAMMAD.

WHEN MUHAMMAD DIED IN 632 ce, HIS SUCCESSOR, THE CALIPH, LED THE DESERT DWELLERS AGAINST THE OUTSIDE WORLD.

WITH FLASHING SCIMITARS AND A PURE, SIMPLE, PROPHETIC MONOTHEISM, THE ARABS SPEEDILY ESTABLISHED AN ISLAMIC EMPIRE THAT EXTENDED FROM ASIA TO NORTH AFRICA.

QUR'AN

IN 711 ce, THEY CROSSED OVER INTO SPAIN AND DEFEATED THE VISIGOTHS. THE **JEWS OF SPAIN,** WHO'D BEEN TREATED FAIRLY BY THE BARBARIANS <u>UNTIL THE VISIGOTH KING BECAME CHRISTIAN</u>...

...WELCOMED THE MUSLIM INVADERS.

B-BUT I THOUGHT WE WERE BUSINESS PARTNERS.

THAT WAS BEFORE I CONVERTED!

THE MUSLIMS, TOLERANT OF CHRISTIANITY AND JUDAISM, WERE QUICK TO MAKE USE OF JEWISH SKILLS.

THE ARABS DEMONSTRATED A PASSION FOR KNOWLEDGE AND CULTURE. BY THE 10TH CENTURY, ISLAMIC SPAIN WAS JAMMED WITH SCHOLARS AND POETS. **FOR THE JEWS IT WAS A GOLDEN AGE OF ACHIEVEMENT.**

JEWISH WRITING HAD ALWAYS PUT GOD AT THE CENTER OF THE UNIVERSE. NOW, THE ARABS INTRODUCED THE JEWS TO A SENSUOUS AND INDIVIDUALISTIC VIEW OF LIFE. POETS WERE THE MOVIE STARS OF MUSLIM SPAIN.

LIFE IS A PEARL IN A GLASS OF WINE, IN THE HAND OF A LOVELY WOMAN.

ART FOR ITS OWN SAKE? NO SUFFERING? WHAT KIND OF PEOPLE ARE THESE ARABS?

THE JEWS ADAPTED THE ARABS' LOVE OF LANGUAGE AND POETRY TO THEIR OWN TRADITIONAL THEMES.

OH, SWEET NIGHTINGALE, FEATHERED EXPRESSION OF BEAUTY, BEFORE GOD'S POWER, BETTER BUTTON YOUR BEAK.

WHILE THE JEWS ADOPTED MANY ARAB WAYS, THEIR SPIRITUAL LIFE WAS GUIDED FROM BABYLONIA. MESSENGERS RAN BACK AND FORTH CARRYING QUESTIONS FROM THE DIASPORA AND ANSWERS, CALLED **RESPONSA,** FROM BABYLONIA.

BY THE 10TH CENTURY, BABYLONIAN POWER WAS FADING, AND **JEWISH AUTHORITY BEGAN A SHIFT TO THE DIASPORA.** A GREAT ITALIAN SCHOLAR, MOSES BEN HANOCH, WAS HIJACKED BY MEDITERRANEAN PIRATES AND ENDED UP IN SPAIN.

IN SPAIN, BEN HANOCH BECAME HEAD OF THE NEW CENTER OF TALMUDIC LEADERSHIP.

**D**URING THE GOLDEN AGE OF SPANISH JEWRY, A RELIGIOUS BATTLE WAS RAGING BETWEEN EASTERN JEWS CALLED KARAITES AND THE INSTITUTIONS OF RABBINIC JUDAISM.

*IN THE OLD DAYS WE HAD A COUNTRY TO FIGHT OVER. NOW WHAT DO WE DO?*

*HOW ABOUT NAME CALLING?*

*TALMUDIST TRICKSTERS!*

*REGRESSIVE FUNDAMENTALISTS!*

**T**HIS BATTLE, FOUGHT ON THE FIELD OF JEWISH SCHOLARSHIP, ACTUALLY LED TO REFORM AND A STRENGTHENING OF THE JEWS' ABILITY TO COPE WITH THE COMING **FEUDAL YEARS**...

...*AS THEY BEGAN TO MAKE THEIR MOVE FROM MEDITERRANEAN AND BYZANTINE CITIES INTO* **CENTRAL EUROPE.**

# TWO PATHS OF THE JEWISH EXPERIENCE

## SEPHARDIM

Jews whose ancestors came from Spain.

## ASHKENAZIM

Jews whose ancestors came from Europe north of Spain and Italy.

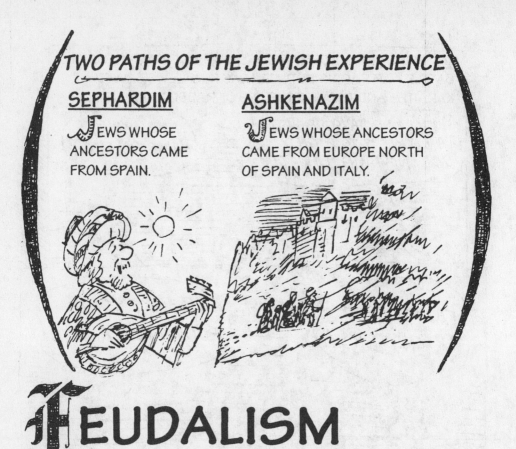

# Feudalism

By the 7th century, the Christian Germanic tribes were settled in what is now France, Germany, and Italy. The nobles ran society. Under them were serfs, knights, and clerics.

The SERFS did all the work.

The KNIGHTS fought other knights.

The CLERGY hung out in the churches.

IN THE 9TH CENTURY, THE JEWS WERE IN CHARLEMAGNE'S EMPIRE IN CENTRAL EUROPE. BY THE 10TH, IN NORTHERN FRANCE. BY 1000, THEY WERE SETTLED ALONG THE RHINE. AND IN THE 11TH, ENGLAND.

NOT AGAIN! I THOUGHT WE LEFT THEM BEHIND IN ROME!

THE JEWS ARRIVED WITH EDUCATION, SKILLS, AND CONTACTS THROUGHOUT THE MEDITERRANEAN WORLD. THEY TURNED THEMSELVES INTO **THE MERCHANT CLASS** OF A BACKWARD EUROPE.

FAIRGROUNDS

I CALL THIS A DEPARTMENT STORE.

SPICES FROM INDIA

WINES FROM ITALY

OILS FROM EGYPT

**L**OCAL OVERLORDS VALUED THE JEWS, GAVE THEM PROTECTION, AND ALLOWED THEM TO GOVERN THEMSELVES BY JEWISH LAW. THE ROMAN CATHOLIC CHURCH, GAINING IN WORLDLY POWER, GRUMBLED AT JEWISH SUCCESSES.

**T**HE CHURCH FROWNED UPON CHRISTIANS LOANING MONEY AT INTEREST. <u>BY DEFAULT, THE JEWS WOULD BECOME THE BANKERS TO CHRISTIAN EUROPE.</u>

THE RESPONSA MESSENGERS DID SHOW UP, BUT IT WAS TOUGH TO RELATE ANSWERS FROM THE SUNNY, POETICAL SOUTH TO THIS COLD, BARBAROUS PLACE.

CHATTER CHATTER

THESE DIETARY LAWS ARE ABOUT GOATS AND CAMELS. WHAT ABOUT DEER, BEAR, AND SQUIRREL?

THEN, A BRILLIANT FRENCH RABBI NICKNAMED RASHI, BORN AROUND 1040, WROTE SIMPLE, CLEAR COMMENTARIES ON THE TORAH. HE GAVE ASHKENAZIC JEWRY A PATH TO THEIR FAITH THAT WOULD SUSTAIN THEM IN HOSTILE TIMES.

OOPS

NOW, WE DON'T NEED RESPONSA. WE CAN STUDY TOGETHER AND FIND OUR OWN WAY.

AROUND 1000, ATTACKS BY MUSLIM FUNDAMENTALIST AND ETHNIC GROUPS BEGAN TO TEAR APART SOPHISTICATED ISLAMIC SPAIN. FROM THE NORTH, CHRISTIAN ARMIES ADVANCED. THE JEWS OF SPAIN, CAUGHT IN THE MIDDLE, STRUGGLED TO SURVIVE.

AS THE CHAOS INCREASED, WANDERING SEPHARDIC POETS KEPT ALIVE THE GOLDEN AGE OF THE JEWS. THEY WROTE LUMINOUSLY OF LOVE AND TREACHERY, JOY AND LONELINESS, AND A MYSTICAL YEARNING FOR THE HOLY LAND.

ENEMY CHAINS BIND THE NIGHTINGALE'S LEGS, IT SEARCHES FOR GOD'S LIGHT, BUT SEES ONLY STARS.

AS THE CHRISTIAN KINGS GRADUALLY CONQUERED SPAIN, SEPHARDIC JEWS BECAME PART OF LATIN CHRISTENDOM, THEIR DIPLOMATIC AND ADMINISTRATIVE SKILLS HELPING SMOOTH THE TAKEOVER.

**THEN, IN 1070,** JERUSALEM, ONCE UNDER BYZANTINE CONTROL, WAS CAPTURED BY TURKS. **THE BYZANTINE EMPEROR APPEALED TO THE POPE FOR HELP.**

DEAR POPE, PLEASE SEND A FEW BRAVE KNIGHTS TO HELP DEFEND CHRISTIAN BYZANTIUM AGAINST THE HEATHENS.

IF THE EMPEROR COULD HAVE SEEN WHAT WOULD HAPPEN NEXT, HE'D HAVE KEPT HIS MOUTH SHUT.

# 7

# CONVERT
# OR ELSE!

## (CRUSADES–INQUISITION)
### 1000s–1500s

# AT THE TURN OF THE MILLENNIUM,

THE CHILDREN OF ABRAHAM WERE SETTLED IN MANY PLACES AND CULTURES AROUND THE GLOBE.

*YOU DON'T LOOK JEWISH.*

*NEITHER DO YOU.*

# IN MEDIEVAL FRANCE AND GERMANY,

JEWS WERE SHOPKEEPERS, ARTISANS, AND MERCHANTS— THE FIRST EUROPEAN MIDDLE CLASS, LIVING AT RELATIVE PEACE WITH THE LOCAL NOBLES AND PEASANTS.

*IT'S WOOL FROM PERSIA—VERY WARM. I CAN LET OUT THE WAIST.*

*I WANT ONE.*

*ME, TOO.*

BUT ONE GROUP CONTINUED TO VIEW THE JEWS AS TROUBLE.

To the Christian Church, the Jews were to be hated. And the church had become more powerful than secular monarchs.

JEWS ARE SINNERS! WHY ELSE WOULD THEY REJECT US?

During feudal times, Europe was full of mysticism and superstition. People believed that angels and devils danced across the land. They used crosses, gargoyles, and images of saints as shields against evil.

WOOOOOOOO BOOO EEOW EEEE SCREEE AAAAA SIN! SIN!

THE SUPERSTITIOUS AND GULLIBLE OF MEDIEVAL EUROPE, *WHO WERE A LOT OF PEOPLE*, WERE QUICK TO SWALLOW THE CHURCH'S PRONOUNCEMENTS.

TO CLEANSE OUR LAND OF SIN, WE MUST PUNISH THOSE WHO DO THE DEVIL'S WORK.

IN 1095, POPE URBAN II CAME UP WITH AN IDEA TO STRENGTHEN THE ROMAN CHURCH BY HELPING BYZANTIUM.

WHAT CAN GO WRONG?

I'M CALLING FOR A RELIGIOUS CRUSADE TO SAVE CONSTANTINOPLE AND RESCUE THE HOLY LAND FROM THE INFIDELS!

# THE CRUSADES

NOBLES AND PEASANTS, WOMEN AND CHILDREN, SAINTS AND CRIMINALS, MAGICIANS AND VISIONARIES, PEOPLE WHO'D NEVER BEEN ANYWHERE IN THEIR WHOLE LIFE DROPPED EVERYTHING TO FOLLOW GOD'S CALL.

113

IN THOSE YEARS OF MADNESS AND DISLOCATION, THE SELF-GOVERNING JEWISH COMMUNITIES OF EUROPEAN AND MEDITERRANEAN WORLDS SEARCHED FOR AN ENLIGHTENED AND FORCEFUL SPIRITUAL LEADER AND GUIDE.

REASON AND LAW ARE SWORD AND SHIELD TO THE JEWS.

ONE OF THE GREAT PHILOSOPHERS AND LEADERS IN JEWISH HISTORY NOW MADE HIS APPEARANCE. HE WAS BORN IN CORDOVA, SPAIN, IN 1135. EVENTUALLY SETTLING IN CAIRO, EGYPT, HE WAS RENOWNED AS A PHYSICIAN AND SCHOLAR.
HE IS KNOWN AS

# MAIMONIDES.

MAIMONIDES WAS NOTED FOR TREATING PSYCHOSOMATIC DISORDERS. . . AND COMPLAINING OF HIS OWN IMAGINED ILLNESSES.

I THINK I AM SICK, THERE-FORE, I AM.

115

**M**AIMONIDES WAS A SCIENTIST WHO BELIEVED THAT THE APPARENTLY MIRACULOUS COULD BE PROVEN BY REASON. HE USED GREEK PHILOSOPHICAL LOGIC TO ANALYZE ALL OF THE CLASSIC JEWISH WORKS.

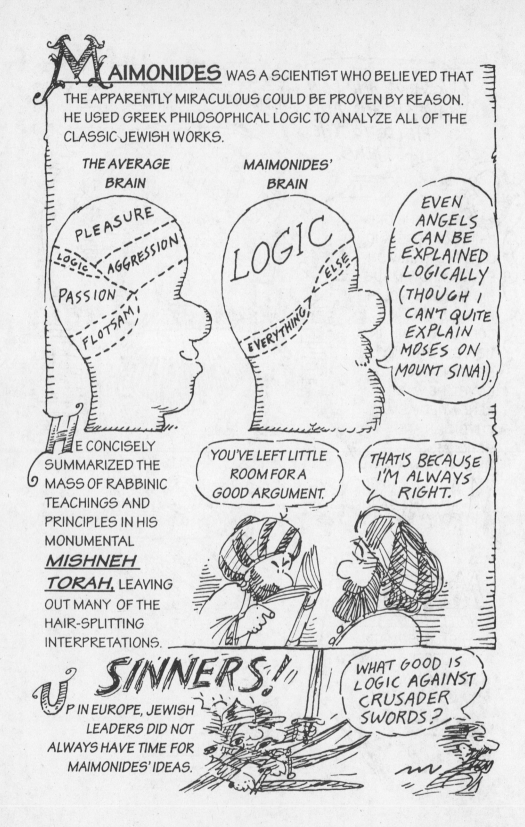

THE AVERAGE BRAIN

PLEASURE · LOGIC · AGGRESSION · PASSION · FLOTSAM

MAIMONIDES' BRAIN

LOGIC · EVERYTHING? · ELSE

EVEN ANGELS CAN BE EXPLAINED LOGICALLY (THOUGH I CAN'T QUITE EXPLAIN MOSES ON MOUNT SINAI).

**H**E CONCISELY SUMMARIZED THE MASS OF RABBINIC TEACHINGS AND PRINCIPLES IN HIS MONUMENTAL **MISHNEH TORAH,** LEAVING OUT MANY OF THE HAIR-SPLITTING INTERPRETATIONS.

YOU'VE LEFT LITTLE ROOM FOR A GOOD ARGUMENT.

THAT'S BECAUSE I'M ALWAYS RIGHT.

**SINNERS!** **U**P IN EUROPE, JEWISH LEADERS DID NOT ALWAYS HAVE TIME FOR MAIMONIDES' IDEAS.

WHAT GOOD IS LOGIC AGAINST CRUSADER SWORDS?

RATIONALISM WAS A HERETICAL AND DANGEROUS CONCEPT IN FEUDAL EUROPE. MANY JEWS TURNED INSTEAD TO A JEWISH TRADITION OF **MYSTICISM** FOR ITS MIRACULOUS POWER TO COMFORT AND PROTECT AGAINST EVIL.

WHERE'D THEY GO.?

DESPITE THE BLOODY CRUSADES, SOME JEWS IN EUROPE AND ENGLAND CONTINUED TO PROSPER BUT ONLY AS THE PROTECTED PROPERTY OF KINGS.

KING AND COMPANY IMPORTERS
SPICES | WINES | OI—

AT THIS TIME, THE PLACE OF JEWISH WOMEN WAS IN THE HOME. BUT, IN BAGHDAD, THERE WAS A WOMAN WHOSE FATHER APPROVED OF HER STUDYING JEWISH LAW. **BAT HA LEVI** WAS NOTED FOR HER SCHOLARSHIP AND BEAUTY. SHE LECTURED FROM BEHIND A SCREEN SO AS NOT TO DISTRACT MALE STUDENTS.

ANY QUESTIONS.?

THE CRUSADES FIZZLED AROUND 1300. THE RELIGIOUS RAMPAGES ACTUALLY LED TO THE DOWNFALL OF BYZANTIUM AND THE DECLINE OF FEUDALISM IN EUROPE. **PEASANTS RETURNED FROM THE CRUSADES AND HEADED FOR THE CITIES.**

WHO WANTS TO BE A SERF ONCE YOU'VE SACKED CONSTANTINOPLE ?!?

THE EX-SERFS SET TO WORK STUDYING THE BUSINESS METHODS OF JEWISH TRADERS.

THEY CALL IT A FREE MARKET ECONOMY.

✓ SUPPLY AND DEMAND
✓ FOREIGN MONEY
✓ GLOBAL MARKETS
BUSINESS HEADACHE

THE SAME CHANGES THAT WOULD IMPROVE CHRISTIAN LIFE LED TO INCREASED HOSTILITY TOWARD THE JEWS. CHRISTIANS MOVED INTO JEWISH BUSINESSES AND FORMED GUILDS THAT EXCLUDED THEM.

LONG LIVE THE CHRISTIAN FREE MARKET!

THE JEWS WERE LEFT WITH **MONEY LENDING,** THE BUSINESS THE CHURCH HATED AND EVERYONE BADLY NEEDED—HOW ELSE TO FINANCE HARVESTS, CATHEDRALS, AND WARS?

LOAN RATES

IN TIME, THE NEW CHRISTIAN BUSINESSMEN GREW ENVIOUS OF THE PROFITS BEING MADE BY JEWISH BANKERS.

DEVIL USURERS!

AGAIN?

120

WITH ALL THE CHANGES, ORDINARY CHRISTIANS WERE BEGINNING TO QUESTION AUTHORITY, AND THE CHURCH AND KINGS WERE GETTING NERVOUS. THEY TURNED ON THE JEWS AND MADE THEM SCAPEGOATS AND TARGETS OF MOB ACTION.

JEWS ARE ALWAYS READING BOOKS...

...SPREADING HERETICAL, RADICAL, SUBVERSIVE IDEAS.

THE JEWS WERE ACCUSED OF BIZARRE ACTS LIKE USING THE BLOOD OF CHRISTIANS TO MAKE PASSOVER MATZOS.

THE TALMUD WAS PUT ON TRIAL FOR BLASPHEMY, FOUND GUILTY, AND BURNED AT THE STAKE.

JEWS WERE FORCED TO WEAR DISTINCTIVE CLOTHING, AND THEIR MOVEMENTS WERE RESTRICTED. THEY BEGAN TO WITHDRAW FROM THE WORLD IN WHICH THEY HAD ONCE BEEN SO ACCOMPLISHED.

BY THE 14TH CENTURY, ENGLAND AND FRANCE ELIMINATED JEWISH INFLUENCE BY OFFICIALLY EXPELLING THE JEWS, WHO MOVED EASTWARD, JOINING ESTABLISHED JEWISH COMMUNITIES IN GERMANY. THEY ARRIVED JUST AS THE BUBONIC PLAGUE HIT EUROPE IN 1348.

COUGH!

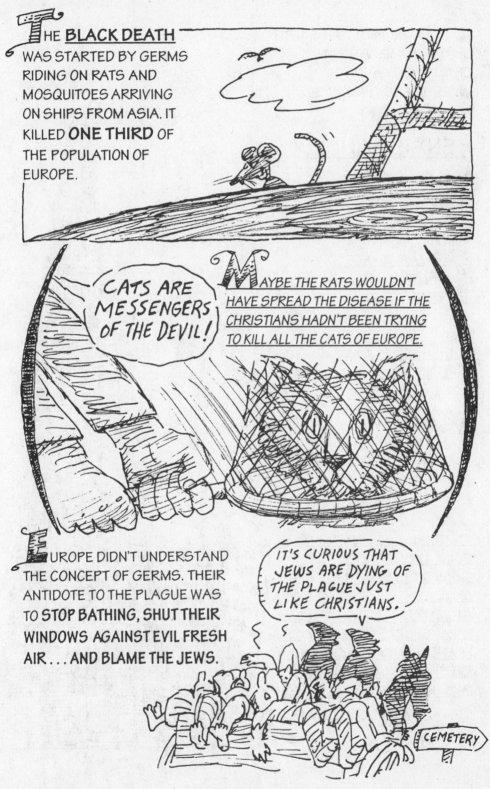

THE **BLACK DEATH** WAS STARTED BY GERMS RIDING ON RATS AND MOSQUITOES ARRIVING ON SHIPS FROM ASIA. IT KILLED **ONE THIRD** OF THE POPULATION OF EUROPE.

CATS ARE MESSENGERS OF THE DEVIL!

MAYBE THE RATS WOULDN'T HAVE SPREAD THE DISEASE IF THE CHRISTIANS HADN'T BEEN TRYING TO KILL ALL THE CATS OF EUROPE.

EUROPE DIDN'T UNDERSTAND THE CONCEPT OF GERMS. THEIR ANTIDOTE TO THE PLAGUE WAS TO **STOP BATHING, SHUT THEIR WINDOWS AGAINST EVIL FRESH AIR . . . AND BLAME THE JEWS.**

IT'S CURIOUS THAT JEWS ARE DYING OF THE PLAGUE JUST LIKE CHRISTIANS.

CEMETERY

**F**ROM THE 14TH TO THE 16TH CENTURY, A NEW SPIRIT OF CURIOSITY AND INVESTIGATION PRODUCED THE <u>ITALIAN RENAISSANCE,</u> A GLORIOUS PERIOD OF CREATIVE EXPLORATION.

**R**ENAISSANCE ITALY WAS MORE TOLERANT OF JEWS, AND YOUNG JEWS FITTED THEMSELVES INTO ITS EXPERIMENTAL LIFE-STYLE.

WHEN IN ROME, WE DO WHAT THE ROMANS DO.

**W**ITH ALL THE FREETHINKING GOING ON IN EUROPE, CHRISTIANS BEGAN TO CRITICIZE CHURCH PRACTICES. A NERVOUS CHURCH SET UP PAPAL COURTS, ORIGINALLY IN FRANCE, TO PUNISH CHRISTIAN REFORMERS (AND JEWISH MYSTICS). IT WAS CALLED THE

**INQUISITION.**

I DON'T LIKE THE SIGHT OF BLOOD SO WE'LL BURN HERETICS AT THE STAKE.

# THE INQUISITION

IN 13TH CENTURY SPAIN, THE CHRISTIAN CLERGY PRESSURED SEPHARDIC JEWS TO CONVERT. THOSE WHO CHOSE TO PRESERVE THEIR WORLD THROUGH CONVERSION WERE CALLED **MARRANOS OR CONVERSOS.** *SOME CONVERTED ONLY OUTWARDLY. IN PRIVATE, THEY REMAINED JEWS.*

JESUS WILL RETURN WHEN ALL JEWS ARE BROUGHT INTO THE CHURCH.

CONVERSOS ROSE TO IMPORTANT POSITIONS IN THE SPANISH STATES, INCLUDING WITHIN THE CHURCH ITSELF. BUT ANTI-CONVERSO JEALOUSY FUELED CIVIL RIOTING IN THE REGION.

THEY'LL BE RUNNING EVERYTHING IF WE DON'T STOP THEM!

# FERDINAND AND ISABELLA'S

MARRIAGE UNIFIED THE SPANISH NATION. THE ROYAL PAIR KICKED OFF THE **SPANISH INQUISITION** IN 1478. MOST OF THE VICTIMS OF THE INQUISITION WOULD BE OF JEWISH HERITAGE.

ANYONE WHO QUESTIONS CHRISTIAN DOGMA IS TOAST, ESPECIALLY CONVERSOS.

THE HEAD INQUISITOR, TORQUEMADA, AND SOME OF THE OTHER INQUISITORS WERE CONVERTS OR OF JEWISH HERITAGE AND **KNEW WELL THE DETAILS OF JEWISH RITUAL.**

YOU DID NOT HAVE SMOKE COMING OUT OF YOUR CHIMNEY ON SATURDAYS. YOU MUST HAVE BEEN OBSERVING THE SABBATH.

YOU WERE HEARD HAVING A PHILOSOPHICAL DISCUSSION, AND YOU NEVER MENTIONED JESUS. YOU HERETIC!

**B**UT THE INQUISITION WAS OUT OF CONTROL. THE VIOLENCE WAS RELENTLESS. THE JAILS OVERFLOWED. THE COST WAS STAGGERING. **FINALLY, FERDINAND ACTED.** ➡

ALL JEWS AND FORMER JEWS ARE EXPELLED FROM SPAIN, LEAVING BEHIND THEIR MONEY, OF COURSE!

**A**S THE JEWS WERE BEING EXPELLED, FERDINAND AND ISABELLA WERE SENDING **CHRISTOPHER COLUMBUS** TO INDIA TO GRAB AWAY THE RICH ASIAN TRADE FROM THE MUSLIMS. COLUMBUS WAS AIDED BY JEWISH MAP MAKERS AND TRANSLATORS.

SUPPOSE THE OCEAN IS TOO WIDE, AND WE CAN'T GET ACROSS?

DON'T WORRY, CHRIS. THE GLOBE IS SMALLER THAN THE GREEKS SAID.

COLUMBUS DIDN'T MAKE IT TO INDIA. INSTEAD...

. . . IN 1492, COLUMBUS SHOWED UP IN AMERICA—THE LAND THAT WOULD BECOME THE MOST IMPORTANT OF DIASPORA DESTINATIONS.

CAPTAIN, THEY DON'T KNOW SPANISH OR ITALIAN.

TRY HEBREW.

THE SEPHARDIC SURVIVORS LEFT SPAIN, **THE LAND THESE GIFTED PEOPLE HAD LIVED IN FOR HUNDREDS OF YEARS.** THEY HEADED FOR ITALY, HOLLAND, NORTH AFRICA, TURKEY, PALESTINE, AND SOUTH AMERICA.

SO, WHERE'RE WE GOING?

I DON'T KNOW, WHERE SHOULD WE GO?

IN THE 15th CENTURY, AS THE JEWS OF SPAIN WERE SCATTERING, THE ASHKENAZI JEWS WERE **MOVING EAST** INTO THE LANDS OF AUSTRIA, POLAND, AND LITHUANIA. THEY WOULD BE WELCOMED BY RULING CLASSES ANXIOUS TO USE THEIR SKILLS TO EXPAND TRADE WITH THE WEST.

NOW WHAT?

I'LL SEE WHAT THE RABBIS SAY.

HELP WANTED
GOOD BENEFITS
Polish Nobility

AT THIS TIME, **JOSEPH CARO,** A SPANISH REFUGEE LIVING IN PALESTINE, SUMMARIZED JEWISH LAW, MAKING IT UNDERSTANDABLE TO THE AVERAGE JEW ON THE MOVE. CARO'S GUIDE WENT WITH THEM AS THEY MOVED INTO THE ERA OF THE **GHETTO** AND **SHTETL.**

FIND ANYTHING?

MAYBE.

# 8

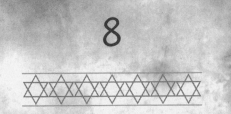

# CAGED

## (GHETTO–SHTETL)
### 1500s–1700s

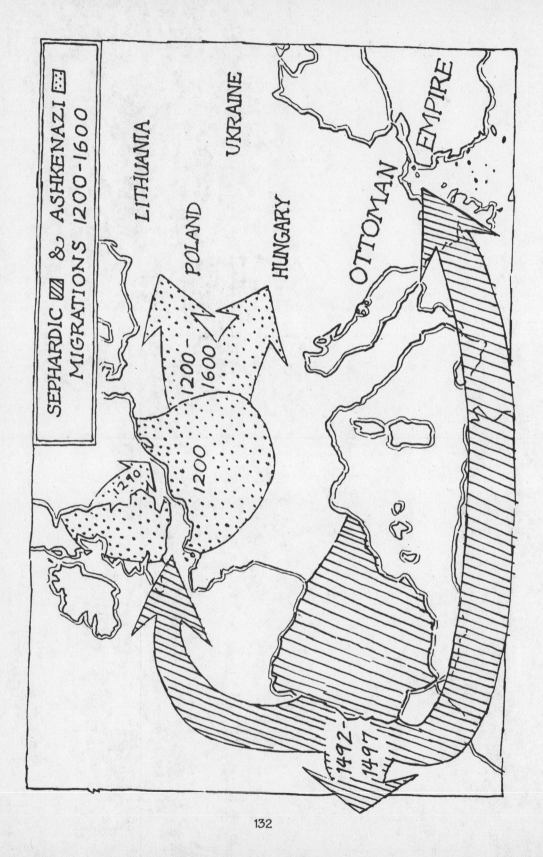

SEPHARDIC ▨ & ASHKENAZI ▦ MIGRATIONS 1200-1600

LITHUANIA

POLAND

UKRAINE

HUNGARY

OTTOMAN EMPIRE

1200–1600

1200

1290

1492–1497

**I**N THE 16TH CENTURY, THE ROMAN CATHOLIC CHURCH FINALLY GOT WHAT IT FEARED—BUT THE JEWS HAD NOTHING TO DO WITH IT. MARTIN LUTHER'S IDEAS FOR RELIGIOUS REFORM LED TO A REVOLT IN WHICH CATHOLICS AND PROTESTANTS SLAUGHTERED EACH OTHER.

**N**EVERTHELESS, AS SOME JEWS MOVED NORTH AND EAST INTO THE WORLD OF SHTETLS, THE MEDIEVAL POWERS FINISHED SEPARATING OTHER JEWS FROM CHRISTIAN LIFE BY PUSHING THEM INTO DEAD-END GHETTOS.

## GHETTO

AN ISOLATED AND OFTEN WALLED-IN SECTION OF A EUROPEAN CITY. ➤

## SHTETL

A SMALL TOWN OR VILLAGE IN RURAL EASTERN EUROPE. ➤

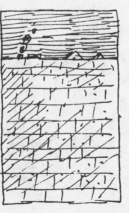

# GHETTO

IN 1516, IN VENICE, THE CHURCH AND LOCAL BUSINESSES FORCED THE JEWS INTO A WALLED AREA THAT HAD BEEN A FOUNDRY CALLED THE GHETTO. AS A PLACE OF JEWISH CONFINEMENT, THE GHETTO MODEL SPREAD ACROSS EUROPE AND NORTH AFRICA.

GHETTO LIFE WAS A HUMILIATING EXISTENCE. THE JEWS STRUGGLED TO MAINTAIN THEIR SAFETY AND DIGNITY. THEY RAN THEIR LIVES BY THE ETHICAL GUIDELINES OF THE TALMUD. THEY CAME OUT TO DO BUSINESS BY DAY. BUT WERE CLOSED IN AT NIGHT.

I WON'T BE LATE.

DESPITE THE RESTRAINTS, JEWS FILLED THEIR LIVES WITH THE RICHNESS OF COMMUNITY THAT HAS ALWAYS CHARACTERIZED THEIR CULTURE. THEY SUPPORTED THEIR POOR, EDUCATED THEIR CHILDREN, AND CELEBRATED THEIR HOLIDAYS AND FESTIVALS.

# GHETTO LIFE

WORE DOWN THE JEWS PSYCHOLOGICALLY AND PHYSICALLY. ORDINARY CHRISTIANS LOOKED AT THE PECULIAR-LOOKING PEOPLE AND COULD NOT IMAGINE THE ACHIEVERS OF EARLIER TIMES.

OUTSIDE THE GHETTO WORLD, SOME JEWS CONTINUED TO BOTH PROSPER AND STAY TRUE TO JEWISH TRADITION.

JEWS WERE ESPECIALLY VALUED BY SLAVERS BECAUSE THERE WAS ALWAYS A JEWISH COMMUNITY WILLING TO RANSOM A JEWISH HOSTAGE.

DONA GRACIA NASI, A CONVERSO, RAN A BUSINESS EMPIRE FROM ITALY AND SECRET CONVERSO ESCAPE ROUTES OUT OF PORTUGAL.

PORTUGUESE WINE

# THE THIRTY-YEARS' WAR BETWEEN CATHOLICS AND PROTESTANTS GOT ROLLING IN 1618.

A RELIGIOUS WAR TURNED POLITICAL AND ECONOMIC AS EUROPE STRUGGLED OUT OF FEUDALISM AND INTO CAPITALISM. WITH NEW ALLIANCES AND NEW ENEMIES SPROUTING EVERYWHERE, EVERY NEW RULER NEEDED MILITARY MIGHT.

BIG ARMIES REQUIRE HARD CASH.

AND HARD CASH REQUIRES SKILLFUL MONEY MANAGING.

RULERS TURNED TO THE PEOPLE WHO WERE RENOWNED FOR THEIR FINANCIAL SKILLS, HAD INTERNATIONAL FAMILY AND COMMUNITY CONNECTIONS, AND, AS DEPENDENTS ON ROYAL PROTECTION, WERE OF LITTLE POLITICAL THREAT.

WHILE MANY JEWS REMAINED TRAPPED IN GHETTOS, OTHERS WERE EMPLOYED BY ROYALTY FOR THEIR SWIFT AND ASSURED FINANCIAL MOVES. THESE MONEY MANAGERS BECAME KNOWN AS **COURT JEWS.**

WE'LL SHIP THE CANNON BY MY COUSIN IN ITALY, BUY GRAIN FROM TURKISH TRADERS I KNOW...

COURT JEWS NEGOTIATED THE TRANSITION FROM A FIXED FINANCIAL SYSTEM TO OPEN INTERNATIONAL MARKETS.

HUH?

WE'LL ISSUE STOCKS, GRANT BILLS OF EXCHANGE, TRADE FOREIGN CURRENCIES...

THEY WIELDED GREAT POWER, LIVED LAVISHLY, AND USED THEIR INFLUENCE TO DEFLECT ATTACKS AWAY FROM THE GHETTOS.

WE'RE NOT FOOLED. AS SOON AS THEY DON'T NEED US, WE'RE HISTORY.

# IN THE 17TH CENTURY, THE PROTESTANT COUNTRIES OF EUROPE OPENED THEIR DOORS TO CAPITALISM AND THE JEWS.

THE NETHERLANDS OFFERED WELCOME AND OPPORTUNITIES TO JEWISH AND CONVERSO REFUGEES.

ENGLAND READMITTED THE JEWS IN THE 1600s.

SO WE'RE IN A WAR WITH FRANCE AND COULD USE YOUR MANAGEMENT SKILLS.

LITTLE HOLLAND MOVED TO THE CENTER OF WORLD TRADE, AND THE JEWISH COMMUNITY OF AMSTERDAM WAS IN THE MIDDLE OF THE ACTION. ONE OF THE DUTCH OVERSEAS TRADING CITIES WAS NAMED NEW AMSTERDAM, LATER,

# NEW YORK.

NEW WORLD

THE JEWS OF ENGLAND HELPED ESTABLISH ENGLISH COLONIES IN THE AMERICAS. AND, ONE DAY, A NEW KIND OF JEWISH SOCIETY WOULD TAKE ROOT THERE.

# SHTETL

LEAVING THE JEWS OF 17TH CENTURY WESTERN EUROPE, WE TRAVEL BACK TO THE 15TH CENTURY TO FOLLOW THE LARGE NUMBERS OF JEWS WHO'D PUSHED EAST INTO THE LANDS OF THE SLAVS.

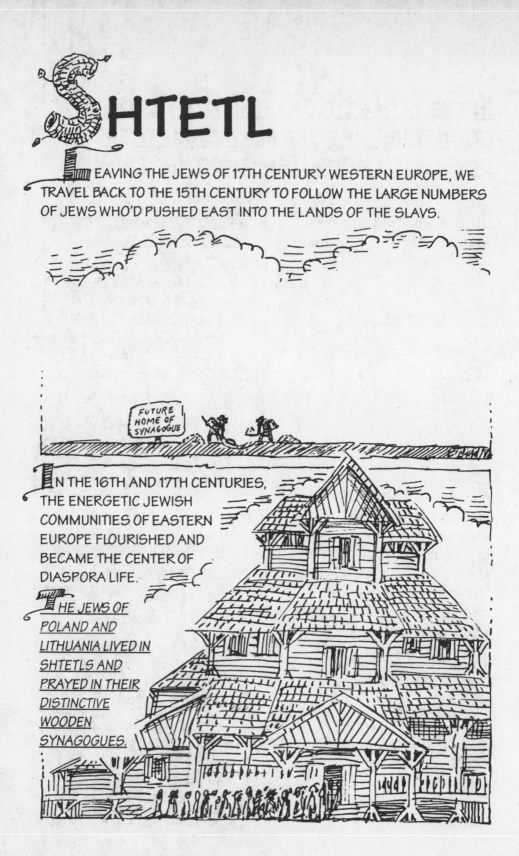

FUTURE HOME OF SYNAGOGUE

IN THE 16TH AND 17TH CENTURIES, THE ENERGETIC JEWISH COMMUNITIES OF EASTERN EUROPE FLOURISHED AND BECAME THE CENTER OF DIASPORA LIFE.

_THE JEWS OF POLAND AND LITHUANIA LIVED IN SHTETLS AND PRAYED IN THEIR DISTINCTIVE WOODEN SYNAGOGUES._

JEWS PROSPERED IN THE INTERNATIONAL LUMBER, FUR, LIVESTOCK, AND LIQUOR BUSINESSES. THEY WERE AGENTS FOR THE NOBILITY, MANAGING ESTATES, GOVERNING SERFS, AND COLLECTING RENTS AND TAXES.

THEY RAN THEIR OWN COMMUNITIES AND WERE GOVERNED BY REGIONAL COUNCILS. THEIR YESHIVAS WERE RENOWNED, AND WOMEN ALSO STUDIED.

TALMUDIC SCHOLARS WERE HONORED ABOVE ALL. BUSINESSMEN IMPROVED THEIR STATUS BY MARRYING THEIR DAUGHTERS TO PROMISING RABBINICAL STUDENTS.

THE PEASANTS WERE TAXED MERCILESSLY BY THE NOBILITY. BUT, WHEN THE PEASANTS ROSE IN REBELLION IN THE MID 1600s, *THEY AIMED THEIR ANGER AT THE ENEMY THEY COULD SEE, AND THE ENEMY OF THEIR CHURCH, THE JEWISH TAX COLLECTORS.*

FURTHER EAST, GREEK ORTHODOX PEASANTS WERE ALSO UNDER THE HEEL OF THE POLISH NOBILITY. LED BY FIERCE BORDER WARRIORS CALLED

# COSSACKS,

THEY LAUNCHED BLOODY ATTACKS AGAINST THEIR TORMENTORS ... AND THE JEWS.

THE POLISH ARMY FELL *BEFORE THE COSSACKS. THE JEWS FOUGHT AND DIED WITH THEM. THE COSSACK KILLING STYLE WAS TO CARVE UP PEOPLE AND ROAST THEM.*

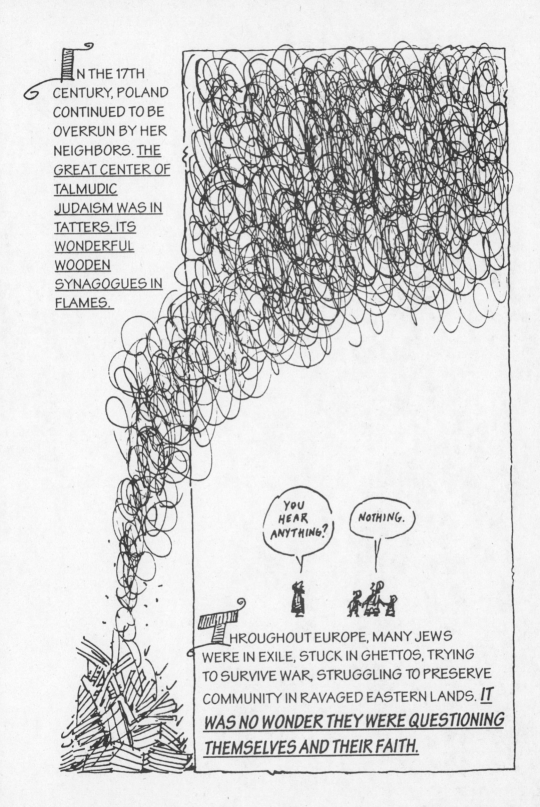

IN THE 17TH CENTURY, POLAND CONTINUED TO BE OVERRUN BY HER NEIGHBORS. <u>THE GREAT CENTER OF TALMUDIC JUDAISM WAS IN TATTERS, ITS WONDERFUL WOODEN SYNAGOGUES IN FLAMES.</u>

YOU HEAR ANYTHING?

NOTHING.

THROUGHOUT EUROPE, MANY JEWS WERE IN EXILE, STUCK IN GHETTOS, TRYING TO SURVIVE WAR, STRUGGLING TO PRESERVE COMMUNITY IN RAVAGED EASTERN LANDS. <u>*IT WAS NO WONDER THEY WERE QUESTIONING THEMSELVES AND THEIR FAITH.*</u>

# 9

# MYSTICS
# AND
# MESSIAHS

## (KABBALAH–HASIDISM)
### 1600s–1700s

THE JEWS OF THE 17TH CENTURY WERE SUFFERING A SPIRITUAL CRISIS. MANY TURNED TO THE COMFORT OF MYSTICISM COMBINED WITH THE IDEA OF A MESSIANIC DELIVERER.

IF ONLY WE KNEW WHERE TO LOOK FOR THE MESSIAH.

THEY SEARCHED THE TEXTS OF THE JEWISH MYSTICAL PHILOSOPHY CALLED

KABBALAH.

THE RABBIS, THE STUDY OF THE TALMUD, AND LOGIC HAVE NOT SAVED US FROM CALAMITY.

BUT CALAMITY CAN ALSO SIGNAL THE COMING OF THE MESSIAH.

147

**K**ABBALAH OFFERED THE JEWS A SOLUTION TO THEIR QUEST.

## HERE IS AN EXTREMELY ABBREVIATED VERSION OF THE KABBALISTIC THEORY OF THE UNIVERSE:

THE DIVINE LIGHT OF GOD WAS CONTAINED IN VESSELS WHICH WERE BROKEN DURING AN APOCALYPTIC BIG BANG. *THE LIGHT SCATTERED AND MIXED WITH ALL THE DEBRIS OF EARTHLY LIFE.*

**F**OR HUMANITY TO ACHIEVE HEAVENLY PERFECTION, ALL THE **DIVINE GLITTER** MUST BE SEPARATED FROM THE DARK PARTS OF HUMAN LIFE AND RESTORED ACCORDING TO GOD'S ORIGINAL PLAN.

ALL THE BASE STUFF

**T**O START THE BALL ROLLING, EACH JEW MUST PERSONALLY GET CLOSE TO GOD THROUGH PRAYER AND THE OBSERVANCE OF THE COMMANDMENTS, **AFTER WHICH THE MESSIAH WILL SHOW UP.**

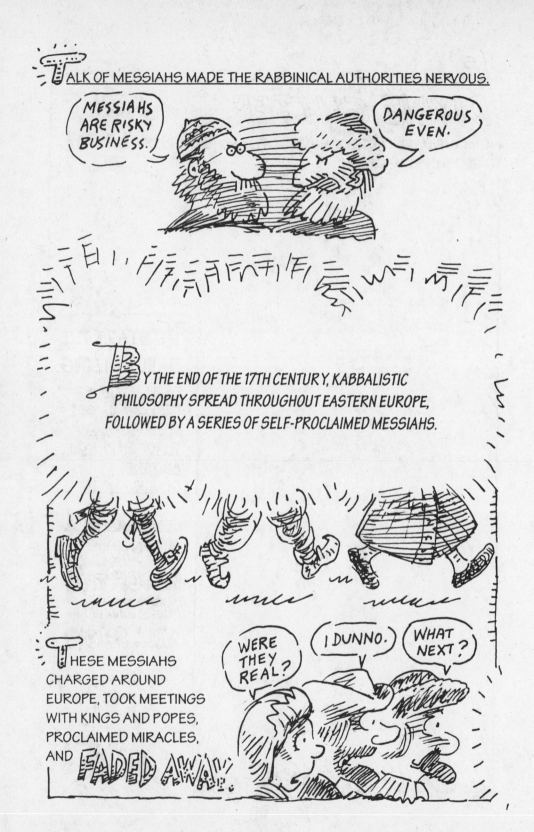

TALK OF MESSIAHS MADE THE RABBINICAL AUTHORITIES NERVOUS.

MESSIAHS ARE RISKY BUSINESS.

DANGEROUS EVEN.

BY THE END OF THE 17TH CENTURY, KABBALISTIC PHILOSOPHY SPREAD THROUGHOUT EASTERN EUROPE, FOLLOWED BY A SERIES OF SELF-PROCLAIMED MESSIAHS.

THESE MESSIAHS CHARGED AROUND EUROPE, TOOK MEETINGS WITH KINGS AND POPES, PROCLAIMED MIRACLES, AND FADED AWAY.

WERE THEY REAL?

I DUNNO.

WHAT NEXT?

MUCH OF EUROPEAN JEWRY THOUGHT THEY'D FOUND THEIR MESSIAH IN **SHABBETAI ZEVI.** BORN IN 1626 IN TURKEY, HE STUDIED KABBALAH AND HEARD **HEAVENLY VOICES.**

I HEAR YOU, LORD.

SHABBETAI ZEVI MARRIED AN ORPHAN OF THE COSSACK MASSACRES, SARAH, AN INTERNATIONALLY KNOWN PROSTITUTE. HE ALSO FORMED A PARTNERSHIP WITH A RABBI, NATHAN OF GAZA, WHO BECAME HIS PRESS AGENT.

SHABBETAI, THE MESSIAH, COME TO HELP RESTORE THE WORLD TO PERFECTION.

I HEAR YOU, LORD.

I HEAR YOU, LORD.

ADORING FOLLOWERS OF ZEVI PACKED THEIR BAGS AND GOT READY TO BE PICKED UP BY ANGELS AND TRANSPORTED TO ZION, THE PROMISED LAND.

ZEVI WAS VERY CONVINCING. EVEN SOME RABBIS HEDGED THEIR BETS.

PROBABLY NO.

MAYBE YES.

THEN SHABBETAI WAS THROWN IN JAIL BY THE TURKISH SULTAN, WHO OFFERED HIM A CHOICE: DEATH OR CONVERSION TO ISLAM. ZEVI CHOSE CONVERSION. ...

I HEAR YOU, ALLAH.

NATHAN DEFENDED HIM, BUT THE ANGELS NEVER SHOWED UP. IT LOOKED LIKE THE MESSIAH WOULDN'T BE COMING AT THAT TIME.

WE NEED A JUDAISM WITH REAL SOUL.

# HASIDISM

AROUND 1730, THE DISCOURAGED JEWS OF EASTERN EUROPE FOUND A NEW VISION OF GOD—IN THE FORESTS OF POLAND.

IN THOSE DAYS, IN GERMANY AND POLAND, FAITH HEALING THRIVED. JEWISH FOLK DOCTORS TENDED THE ORDINARY PEOPLE WITH HERBS, PRAYERS, AND AMULETS. THEY WERE CALLED **BAALEI SHEM.**

ONE SUCH FAITH HEALER WAS **ISRAEL BEN ELIEZER,** BORN IN 1700 IN POLAND, A PERFORMER OF MIRACLES AND A CHARISMATIC TEACHER.

SRAEL BEN ELIEZER, CALLED THE **BAAL SHEM TOV,** INTRODUCED THE DOCTRINE OF **<u>HASIDISM.</u>** HE PREACHED THAT THE SACRED WAS FOUND IN EVERYDAY LIFE, THAT EACH PERSON COULD FEEL *GOD'S* RADIANCE AND SAVE THE WORLD THROUGH HIS OR HER JOYOUS DEVOTION.

SHAKE IT, BUT DON'T BREAK IT.

THE DISCOURAGED AND OPPRESSED JOINED HIM IN ECSTATIC AND PRAYERFUL SINGING, DANCING, AND STORYTELLING. WHEN HE DIED, THE BAAL SHEM TOV'S STUDENTS SPREAD HIS TEACHINGS THROUGHOUT POLAND AND UKRAINE.

AT THE CENTER OF EACH NEW HASIDIC COMMUNITY WAS A BELOVED **REBBE,** WHO SURROUNDED HIS FOLLOWERS WITH HIS EXULTANT SPIRIT AND HELPED THEM FACE THE DANGEROUS OUTSIDE WORLD.

A REBBE WAS A BIT HIGHER THAN ORDINARY PEOPLE, BUT NOT REALLY A MESSIAH, SO THERE COULD BE LOTS OF THEM.

ONE FAMOUS REBBE WAS A WOMAN, HANNAH RACHEL, WHO PERFORMED THE SAME RELIGIOUS OBLIGATIONS AS THE MEN.

THE RABBINIC ESTABLISHMENT BELIEVED THAT HASIDISM UNDERMINED JEWISH LAW!

TALMUDIC STUDY IS SERIOUS! WHY ARE THEY DANCING?

THE GREAT TALMUDIC SCHOLAR, THE GAON OF VILNA, LITHUANIA, CONDEMNED HASIDISM.

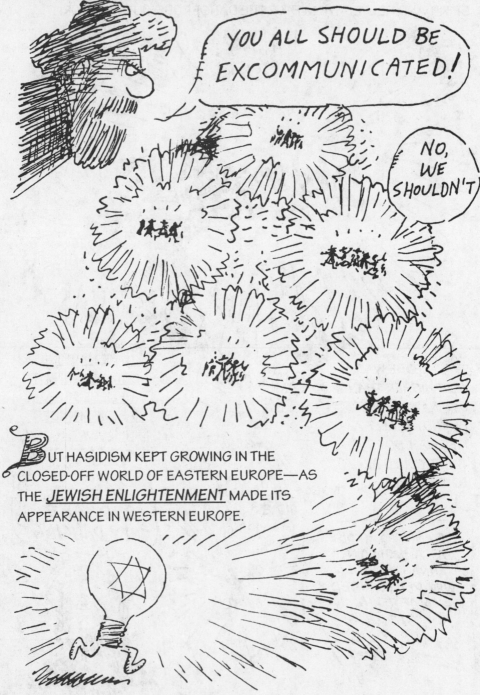

YOU ALL SHOULD BE EXCOMMUNICATED!

NO, WE SHOULDN'T

BUT HASIDISM KEPT GROWING IN THE CLOSED-OFF WORLD OF EASTERN EUROPE—AS THE *JEWISH ENLIGHTENMENT* MADE ITS APPEARANCE IN WESTERN EUROPE.

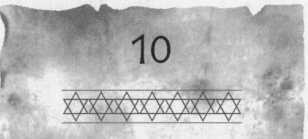

# 10

# GOD,
# THE CLOCK
# MAKER

## (ENLIGHTENMENT–HASKALAH)
## 1700s–1800s

# IN THE 18TH CENTURY, THE ENLIGHTENMENT LIT UP WESTERN EUROPE.

THE PHILOSOPHIES OF ANCIENT GREECE AND ROME, A SCIENTIFIC SEARCH FOR TRUTH, AND A PASSION FOR MOTHER NATURE SWEPT AWAY MEDIEVAL THOUGHT.

IDEAS OF INDIVIDUAL EQUALITY REPLACED RULE BY DIVINE RIGHT. FOR THE JEWS, EQUALITY HAD A FAMILIAR RING.

IN THE 1700's, THESE IDEAS STARTED TO BREAK DOWN THE GHETTO WALLS. THE JEWS, PHYSICALLY AND EMOTIONALLY TRAPPED INSIDE, BEGAN TO CLIMB OUT.

REMEMBER MOSES AND THE SLAVES?

A SALON JEW WHO WAS INSTRUMENTAL IN HELPING THE JEWS ADJUST WAS **MOSES MENDELSSOHN,** AN ODD-LOOKING LITTLE MAN, BORN IN 1729. MOSES HAD TALKED HIS WAY INTO BERLIN, WHERE HE BECAME AN IMPORTANT PHILOSOPHER AND CRITIC.

FORGET MIRACLES—THEY'RE TOO MEDIEVAL. JUDAISM IS ABOUT LAWS.

MENDELSSOHN TRIED TO EXPLAIN JUDAISM TO THE GERMANS AND THE ENLIGHTENMENT TO THE JEWS.

HE SAID WE CAN KEEP OUR JEWISH TRADITIONS IF WE'RE NOT TOO OBVIOUS ABOUT IT.

BUT FOR MANY GERMANS, JEWS WERE STRANGE AND SCARY.

DEVILISH PEOPLE.

THE GERMANS WANTED TO MAKE THE JEWS LESS JEWISH. THEY ASSIGNED GERMAN NAMES TO THE ASHKENAZIM.

IT'S FOR TAX PURPOSES.

MY NAME WAS YAAKOV BEN MOSES, NOW I'M FRANZ KLEIN.

BETTER THAN WHAT THEY GAVE ME: ESELKOPF (DONKEY'S HEAD).

DESPITE THE PREJUDICE OF CHRISTIANS AND THE PROTESTS OF RABBIS, YOUNG GHETTO JEWS EMBRACED THE ENLIGHTENMENT.

I'M NOT WAITING FOR THE MESSIAH ANYMORE.

I SHAVED MY BEARD.

I'M LEARNING HOW TO PLAY CARDS.

THE MONARCHS OF EUROPE WERE TERRIFIED BY THE ENLIGHTENMENT'S IDEA THAT ORDINARY PEOPLE HAD RIGHTS.

IF THEY HAVE NO BREAD, LET THEM EAT CAKE!

AND THE JEWS WERE SWEPT UP IN THE TIDAL WAVE THAT WAS THE FRENCH REVOLUTION

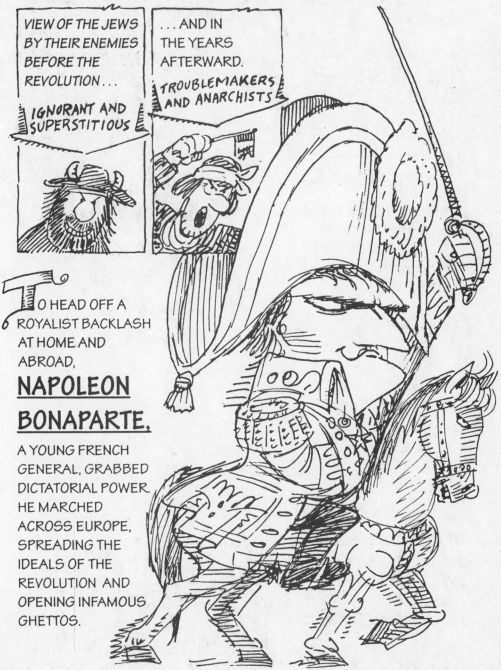

THE FRENCH REVOLUTION WAS AN OPPRESSED PEOPLE'S REVOLT AGAINST THE POWER AND PRIVILEGE OF ARISTOCRACY AND CHURCH. *AFTER THE BASTILLE WAS STORMED IN 1789, THE JEWS GOT EQUAL MEMBERSHIP IN THE NEW FRENCH REPUBLIC—MORE OR LESS.*

VIEW OF THE JEWS BY THEIR ENEMIES BEFORE THE REVOLUTION...

IGNORANT AND SUPERSTITIOUS

...AND IN THE YEARS AFTERWARD.

TROUBLEMAKERS AND ANARCHISTS

TO HEAD OFF A ROYALIST BACKLASH AT HOME AND ABROAD,

**NAPOLEON BONAPARTE,**

A YOUNG FRENCH GENERAL, GRABBED DICTATORIAL POWER. HE MARCHED ACROSS EUROPE, SPREADING THE IDEALS OF THE REVOLUTION AND OPENING INFAMOUS GHETTOS.

163

**N**APOLEON BROUGHT TOGETHER JEWISH NOTABLES AND ASKED THEM A LOT OF QUESTIONS.

HOW DO YOU FEEL ABOUT INTER-MARRIAGE?

DO YOU CONSIDER YOURSELF FRENCH?

WHAT POLICE POWERS DO RABBIS HAVE?

**B**ASED ON THEIR ANSWERS, NAPOLEON ANNOUNCED THAT **JUDAISM WASN'T SUBVERSIVE, IT WAS JUST ANOTHER RELIGION.**

THE POINT IS, WE EXPECT CONFORMITY TO THE FRENCH STATE.

**A** DUTCH JEW, **BARUCH SPINOZA,** BORN IN 1632, BUT NOT FULLY APPRECIATED UNTIL THE 1800s, WAS A TRAILBLAZER FOR JEWISH ENLIGHTENMENT THINKERS.

HE SAYS HE'S NOT SURE WHO WROTE THE BIBLE!

SPINOZA

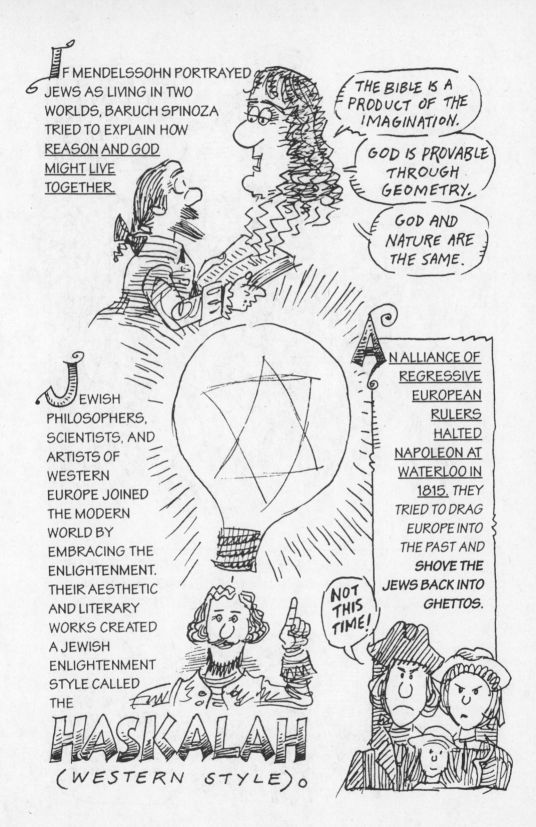

IF MENDELSSOHN PORTRAYED JEWS AS LIVING IN TWO WORLDS, BARUCH SPINOZA TRIED TO EXPLAIN HOW <u>REASON</u> AND GOD MIGHT <u>LIVE</u> TOGETHER.

THE BIBLE IS A PRODUCT OF THE IMAGINATION.

GOD IS PROVABLE THROUGH GEOMETRY.

GOD AND NATURE ARE THE SAME.

JEWISH PHILOSOPHERS, SCIENTISTS, AND ARTISTS OF WESTERN EUROPE JOINED THE MODERN WORLD BY EMBRACING THE ENLIGHTENMENT. THEIR AESTHETIC AND LITERARY WORKS CREATED A JEWISH ENLIGHTENMENT STYLE CALLED THE

HASKALAH
(WESTERN STYLE).

AN ALLIANCE OF <u>REGRESSIVE</u> <u>EUROPEAN</u> <u>RULERS</u> <u>HALTED</u> <u>NAPOLEON</u> AT <u>WATERLOO</u> IN <u>1815.</u> THEY TRIED TO DRAG EUROPE INTO THE PAST AND *SHOVE THE JEWS BACK INTO GHETTOS.*

NOT THIS TIME!

AT THIS TIME, THE ROTHSCHILD BANKING FAMILY WAS GROWING STRONG FINANCING FIRST NAPOLEON AND THEN THE HOLY ALLIANCE.

SOON WE'LL ALSO FUND JEWISH AGRICULTURAL EXPERIMENTS IN PALESTINE.

THE COMMON PEOPLE OF EUROPE WEREN'T ABOUT TO GIVE UP THE IDEALS OF EQUALITY AND NATIONALISM AND GO BACK TO FEUDAL TIMES. BY 1848, MOST OF EUROPE WAS AFLAME WITH REVOLUTION.

A JEWISH ROLE MODEL OF PROTEST AGAINST POLITICAL OPPRESSION WAS THE ACERBIC POET HEINRICH HEINE.

I DO NOT TRUST THESE PRUSSIANS... PIETISTIC HEROES OF THE SPIC AND SPAN UNIFORM, WITH THEIR... CORPORAL'S CLUBS DIPPED INTO HOLY WATER...

DURING THE 1800s, IN WESTERN EUROPE, JEWS FOUGHT ALONGSIDE CHRISTIANS TO DEFEAT THE AUTOCRATIC HOLY ALLIANCE. AS THE NEWLY INDEPENDENT COUNTRIES OPENED THEIR DOORS, JEWS WERE FREE TO BECOME SECULAR CITIZENS OF THE MODERN WORLD.

THE JEWS OF THE HASKALAH WERE ESPECIALLY DRAWN TO THE GERMAN LOVE FOR CULTURE AND SCHOLARLY DISCIPLINE. TO BLEND INTO GERMAN SOCIETY, THEY SANITIZED THEIR OWN RELIGIOUS SERVICES. IT WAS THE RISE OF THE **JEWISH REFORM MOVEMENT.**

IN THE 1800s, INDUSTRY BOOMED, MATERIALISM INCREASED, INTERNATIONAL BANKING GREW, AND A HUGE WORKING CLASS WAS CREATED. **_FOR THE JEWS, IT WAS A TIME OF OPPORTUNITY._**

JEWS WERE INFLUENTIAL IN INTERNATIONALIZING FINANCE. (PEOPLE HAD NEVER BEFORE INVESTED IN <u>FOREIGN</u> CAPITAL.)

JEWS WERE AMONG THE ORGANIZERS HELPING LABORING PEOPLE STAND UP TO FACTORY OWNERS INTERESTED ONLY IN PROFIT.

SOME GERMAN JEWS SAILED FOR THE UNITED STATES AND JOINED THE PIONEER MOVE WEST. THEIR PACKS WOULD GROW INTO WAGONS AND THEIR WAGONS INTO DEPARTMENT STORES.

ASKALAH THINKERS DEVELOPED PHILOSOPHIES BASED ON THE IDEAS OF FREEDOM, RATIONALISM, AND SCIENCE. TWO IMPORTANT THINKERS WERE KARL MARX AND SIGMUND FREUD.

IN ENGLAND, FRANCE, AND GERMANY, JEWS DID GROUNDBREAKING WORK IN EVERY AREA OF MATHEMATICS, THE SCIENCES, AND ESPECIALLY MEDICINE. THEY PIONEERED THE IDEA OF THE EXISTENCE OF MICROSCOPIC CARRIERS OF DISEASE.

THEY'RE CALLED GERMS.

AS THE JEWISH ENLIGHTENMENT MADE ITS WAY EAST, SHTETL DWELLERS OF POLAND AND RUSSIA WOULD ALSO CREATE A HASKALAH. *BUT THEIRS WOULD NOT BE A BREAK WITH THE PAST. IT WOULD BE A SEARCH INTO IT.*

JEWISH TRADITION

BACK IN THE LATE 1700s, RUSSIA WAS RULED BY **CATHERINE THE GREAT.** ALONG WITH HER POLISH LAND GRAB, SHE ACQUIRED A HUGE NUMBER OF JEWS. SHE RESTRICTED THEM TO AN AREA OF POLAND, LITHUANIA, AND UKRAINE CALLED THE PALE OF SETTLEMENT.

IN THE WEST, JEWS MAY BE GREAT SCIENTISTS, BUT, HERE, THEY'RE DEVILS!

THE JEWS, ISOLATED IN THEIR RURAL SHTETLS, REMAINED STUCK IN THEIR CULTURAL PAST.

IF IT WAS OKAY FOR MY GRANDFATHER, IT'S OKAY FOR MY GRANDSON.

IN 1812, NAPOLEON BONAPARTE INVADED RUSSIA, INTRODUCED THE IDEA OF REVOLUTION, AND ALMOST FROZE TO DEATH.

R-R-RETREAT!

THE CZARS PRETENDED TO BE OPEN TO ENLIGHTENMENT IDEAS BUT CONTINUED TO OPPRESS THE SERFS. THEY PUSHED JEWISH CHILDREN INTO STATE SCHOOLS AND THE MILITARY HOPING THEY WOULD ASSIMILATE AND DISAPPEAR AS JEWS.

# HASKALAH (EASTERN STYLE)

CZAR ALEXANDER II INTRODUCED A BRIEF PERIOD OF REFORM TO RUSSIA AND, IN 1861, FREED THE SERFS. YOUNG JEWS, INFLUENCED BY WESTERN IDEAS, REBELLED AGAINST THEIR RIGID SHTETL LIFE AND JOINED A RUSSIAN ARTISTIC AND CULTURAL WORLD.

SO, WE'LL LIVE BY OUR WITS.

THESE EASTERN JEWISH WRITERS AND POETS BEGAN TO WRITE TALES OF THE JEWISH CONDITION FULL OF HUMOR, PASSION, AND WARMTH. _THEY CHANGED THE IMAGE OF JEWS FROM ODD, ROBED MYSTICS TO ENERGETIC MUSCLE-AND-BLOOD PEOPLE._

THEY DEVELOPED TWO LITERATURES. IN HEBREW, THEY WROTE OF JEWISH RENEWAL AND LONGING FOR THE LAND OF ABRAHAM. THEY EXCITED JEWS WITH STORIES OF _SOCIAL REBELLION, PHYSICAL LABOR, AND POLITICAL NATIONALISM._

THE OTHER LANGUAGE WAS YIDDISH, THE FOLK LANGUAGE PIECED TOGETHER BY EARLIER JEWS AS THEY MADE THEIR WAY ACROSS EUROPE. _HASKALAH YIDDISH WRITING ALLOWED JEWS TO LAUGH AT THEMSELVES AND TOLD THEM IT WAS OKAY WITH GOD IF THEY LEFT THE SHTETL._

ONE OF THE WRITERS WAS **SHOLEM ALEICHEM** WHOSE WORK CELEBRATED THE SADNESS, IRONY, ZANINESS, AND HOPE OF THE SHTETL WORLD. HE INVENTED TEVYE, THE ANTI-HEROIC JEWISH HERO, WHO CRITICIZED AND LOVED GOD.

GOD SENT TWO BOATS TO SAVE US. SURELY ONE WOULD HAVE BEEN ENOUGH.

DILEMMA  UNCERTAINTY

IF GOD WANTED IT DIFFERENTLY, IT WOULD HAVE BEEN. YET, WOULD IT HAVE BEEN SO BAD IF IT WERE DIFFERENT? THANKS BE TO GOD.

**M**EANWHILE, RUSSIA WAS FULL OF OPPRESSED PEASANTS AND FACTORY WORKERS, REBELLIOUS MINORITIES, GREEDY OFFICIALS, AND DEADLY SECRET POLICE. *IN 1881,* SOMEONE BLEW UP CZAR ALEXANDER II. THE RUSSIAN ENLIGHTENMENT WAS OVER.

**D**ISCOURAGED YOUNG JEWS JOINED OTHER DESPERATE RUSSIANS THREATENING VIOLENCE AGAINST THE STATE. THE GOVERNMENT ATTEMPTED TO DISTRACT THE PEOPLE BY BLAMING THE JEWS. *THEY INSTIGATED BLOODY ATTACKS, CALLED* **POGROMS,** *AGAINST THEM.*

IT'S THE JEWS' FAULT THAT YOU HAVE NO JOBS AND NO BREAD.

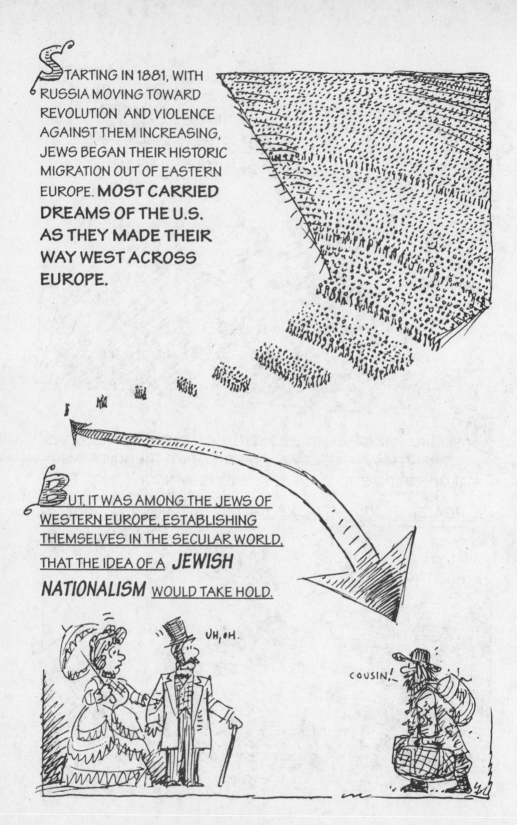

STARTING IN 1881, WITH RUSSIA MOVING TOWARD REVOLUTION AND VIOLENCE AGAINST THEM INCREASING, JEWS BEGAN THEIR HISTORIC MIGRATION OUT OF EASTERN EUROPE. **MOST CARRIED DREAMS OF THE U.S. AS THEY MADE THEIR WAY WEST ACROSS EUROPE.**

BUT, IT WAS AMONG THE JEWS OF WESTERN EUROPE, ESTABLISHING THEMSELVES IN THE SECULAR WORLD, THAT THE IDEA OF A *JEWISH NATIONALISM* WOULD TAKE HOLD.

UH, OH.

COUSIN!

# 11

# TRAVEL PLANS

### (ZION)
#### 1800s–1900s

IN THE 1800'S, WESTERN EUROPEAN JEWS BELIEVED THE ENLIGHTENMENT WAS THEIR TICKET TO **EQUALITY IN THE MODERN AGE.**

INSTEAD, THEY FOUND THEMSELVES IN POSITION TO BE ITS SCAPEGOATS.

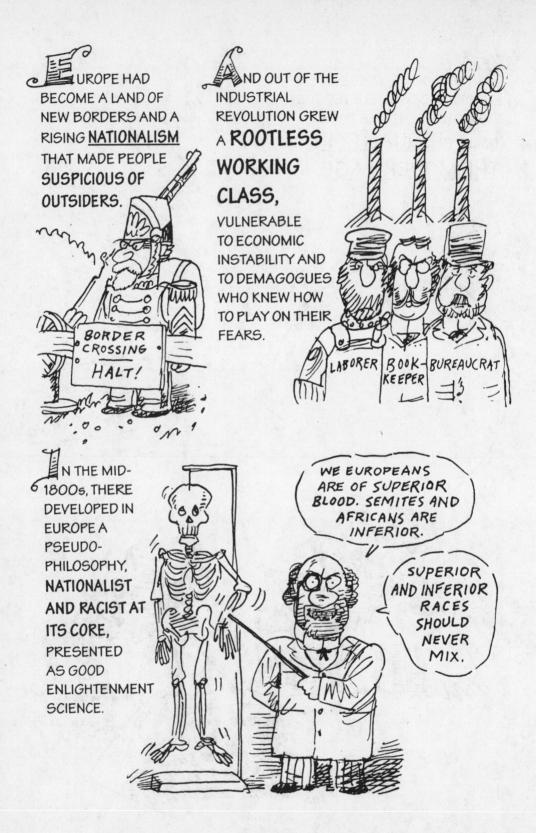

EUROPE HAD BECOME A LAND OF NEW BORDERS AND A RISING **NATIONALISM** THAT MADE PEOPLE **SUSPICIOUS OF OUTSIDERS.**

BORDER CROSSING HALT!

AND OUT OF THE INDUSTRIAL REVOLUTION GREW A **ROOTLESS WORKING CLASS,** VULNERABLE TO ECONOMIC INSTABILITY AND TO DEMAGOGUES WHO KNEW HOW TO PLAY ON THEIR FEARS.

LABORER BOOK-KEEPER BUREAUCRAT

IN THE MID-1800s, THERE DEVELOPED IN EUROPE A PSEUDO-PHILOSOPHY, **NATIONALIST AND RACIST AT ITS CORE,** PRESENTED AS GOOD ENLIGHTENMENT SCIENCE.

WE EUROPEANS ARE OF SUPERIOR BLOOD. SEMITES AND AFRICANS ARE INFERIOR.

SUPERIOR AND INFERIOR RACES SHOULD NEVER MIX.

**THE JEWS OF WESTERN EUROPE** WERE SUCCESSFUL AND INFLUENTIAL. OFTEN LIBERAL AND INTERNATIONALIST, THEY WERE TARGETED AS UNTRUSTWORTHY BY CONSERVATIVE LEADERS.

IF THE SEMITES ARE INFERIOR, HOW COME THE JEWS ARE SO ACCOMPLISHED?

BECAUSE THEY CHEAT!

**YOUNG JEWS OF EASTERN EUROPE** WERE JOINING RADICAL SOCIALIST MOVEMENTS FIGHTING THE CZARS, FUELING MORE ANTI-JEWISH FEELINGS.

CAPITALIST OR COMMUNIST, JEWS ARE TROUBLEMAKERS.

**S**OME PEOPLE BEGAN TO BLEND THE IDEA OF RACIAL SUPERIORITY WITH THE IMAGE OF A EUROPEAN SUPERMAN WHO WAS BEYOND MORAL RIGHT AND WRONG.

181

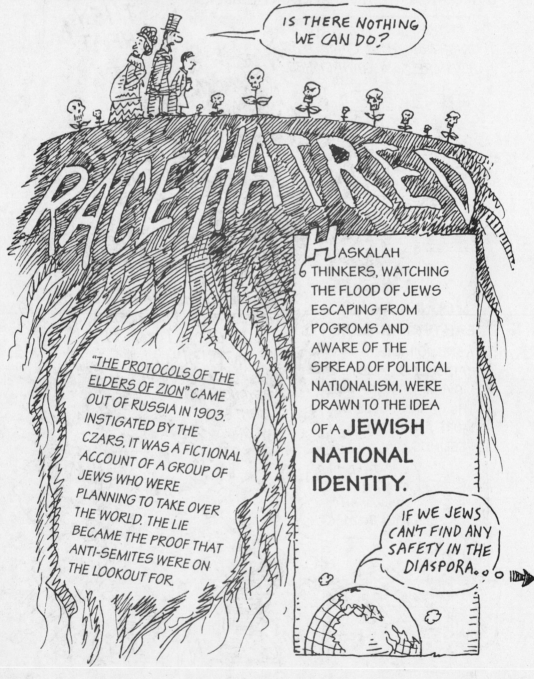

HATRED OF ENTIRE GROUPS OF PEOPLE—MINORITIES, FOREIGNERS, OUTSIDERS—WAS TAKING ROOT ACROSS EUROPE. PROMINENT AMONG THEM WERE THE JEWS. CAPITALIST OR COMMUNIST, SECULAR OR RELIGIOUS, EVERY JEW WAS NOW TAINTED AT BIRTH.

IS THERE NOTHING WE CAN DO?

RACE HATRED

"THE PROTOCOLS OF THE ELDERS OF ZION" CAME OUT OF RUSSIA IN 1903. INSTIGATED BY THE CZARS, IT WAS A FICTIONAL ACCOUNT OF A GROUP OF JEWS WHO WERE PLANNING TO TAKE OVER THE WORLD. THE LIE BECAME THE PROOF THAT ANTI-SEMITES WERE ON THE LOOKOUT FOR.

HASKALAH THINKERS, WATCHING THE FLOOD OF JEWS ESCAPING FROM POGROMS AND AWARE OF THE SPREAD OF POLITICAL NATIONALISM, WERE DRAWN TO THE IDEA OF A **JEWISH NATIONAL IDENTITY.**

IF WE JEWS CAN'T FIND ANY SAFETY IN THE DIASPORA...

...MAYBE WE SHOULDN'T WAIT FOR GOD. MAYBE WE SHOULD TAKE OURSELVES HOME.

ZIONISM BECAME THE NAME FOR THE MOVEMENT WHOSE GOAL WAS THE RETURN OF THE JEWISH PEOPLE TO ZION, THE SUBLIME NAME FOR JERUSALEM.

ALL OVER EUROPE, THE THOUGHTS OF JEWISH NATIONALIST DREAMERS BEGAN TO TURN TOWARD THE PLACE THEY'D OFFICIALLY LEFT 2,000 YEARS AGO, PALESTINE.

OTTOMAN PALESTINE WAS A POOR LAND INHABITED BY ARAB TRIBES AND A FEW RELIGIOUS JEWS. SHTETL PIONEERS, ISRAEL'S FOUNDING FATHERS, BEGAN A MOVE TO THE THE LAND OF THEIR ANCESTORS TO BUILD A NEW SOCIETY.

IN 1893, ZIONISM WAS INADVERTENTLY GIVEN A BOOST WHEN A FRENCH OFFICER, MAJOR ESTERHAZY, ATTEMPTED TO SELL MILITARY SECRETS TO GERMANY. THE PLOT WAS DISCOVERED, BUT A JEWISH OFFICER, **ALFRED DREYFUS,** WAS CONVICTED OF THE CRIME.

GUILTY!

THE EVIDENCE WAS QUESTIONABLE, AND, LED BY **EMILE ZOLA,** FRENCH INTELLECTUALS ACCUSED THE GOVERNMENT OF ANTI-SEMITISM. IRONICALLY, THE UPROAR KICKED OFF **ANTI-SEMITIC RIOTS** THROUGHOUT FRANCE.

DREYFUS WAS FRAMED!

ARREST ZOLA!

JEWS ARE TROUBLEMAKERS!

JEWS ARE EVIL!

UNLIKE THE GHETTO YEARS, JEWS FOUGHT BACK PUBLICLY, EVEN USING THE NEW MEDIUM OF PHOTOGRAPHY TO INFLUENCE OPINION.

ANTI-SEMITISM WAS BECOMING ACCEPTABLE IN EUROPEAN SOCIETY. GERMANY, ESPECIALLY, SAW JEWS AS BIG CITY CONSPIRATORS COME TO INFECT THEIR PROUD "FOLK" CULTURE.

A CENTER OF STRONG ANTI-JEWISH FEELING WAS VIENNA, AUSTRIA. VIENNA WAS ALSO THE HOME OF TALL, ELEGANT

## THEODOR HERZL,

FASHIONABLE JOURNALIST AND PLAYWRIGHT, AND SECULAR JEW.

AS A YOUNG MAN, HERZL WAS DRAWN TO GERMAN NATIONALISM AND STRUGGLED WITH HIS NEGATIVE FEELINGS TOWARD JEWS.

ONLY CONVERSION WILL SAVE JEWS FROM THEIR OWN BAD HABITS,

GERMAN FLAG

SENT TO PARIS TO COVER THE DREYFUS TRIAL, HERZL WAS SHAKEN BY THE ANTI-SEMITIC OUTCRY FROM SUPPOSEDLY LIBERAL FRANCE.

ALL JEWS ARE GUILTY!

IN A DRAMATIC TURNAROUND, HERZL FACED UP TO HIS JEWISH IDENTITY AND WAS SWEPT UP IN A ROMANTIC VISION OF A JEWISH NATIONAL HOME.

IF JEWS AREN'T WANTED IN EUROPEAN SOCIETY, THEN...

# ZIONISM BECAME HERZL'S OBSESSION.

HE TRAVELED ACROSS EUROPE, WRITING, SPEAKING, PRESSURING INFLUENTIAL JEWS AND NON-JEWS, LOOKING FOR MONEY AND SUPPORT FOR HIS DREAM.

...JEWS MUST HAVE A COUNTRY OF THEIR OWN.

**HERZL QUICKLY LEARNED** WHAT MOST POWERFUL AND INTELLECTUAL, RELIGIOUS AND NON-RELIGIOUS, WESTERN AND EASTERN EUROPEAN JEWS AND NON-JEWS THOUGHT OF HIS IDEA.

**H**ERZL FOUND HIS COMMITMENT AMONG THE POOR SHTETL DWELLERS, STUDENTS, AND SEPHARDIM, SOME OF WHOM SAW HIM AS A MESSIANIC FIGURE COME TO LEAD THEM TO A BETTER WORLD.

ONE WHO CAME TO HEAR HIM SPEAK WAS A POLISH TEN-YEAR-OLD NAMED DAVID BEN-GURION

**I**N 1897, HERZL ORGANIZED AN INTERNATIONAL CONFERENCE OF JEWS. IT WAS A HUGE SUCCESS AND STARTED THE WORLD ZIONIST ORGANIZATION. HERZL WAS NOW AT THE HEAD OF A WORLDWIDE MOVEMENT DEVOTED TO THE CREATION OF A JEWISH HOMELAND.

**H**ERZL KEPT FLATTERING, BLUFFING, AND CAJOLING THOSE IN POWER. BUT WEALTHY JEWS, HEADS OF STATE, AND THE TURKISH SULTAN CONTINUED TO REFUSE POLITICAL SUPPORT.

I SEE A SHINING NEW WORLD FULL OF THE LATEST TECHNOLOGIES WITH DEPARTMENT STORES AND HEALTH CLUBS WHERE ARABS AND JEWS WORK TOGETHER... **ARE YOU LISTENING TO ME?**

NO.

NO.

NO.

**H**ERZL DIED AT 44, IN 1904. HIS HEALTH WAS BROKEN, HIS MOVEMENT *STRUGGLING TO SURVIVE.*

WHICH LANGUAGE WOULD WE SPEAK IN?

WILL WE BE A POLITICAL STATE OR A CULTURE WITHIN AN ARAB STATE?

I DON'T SEE WHY PALESTINE WAS BETTER THAN CYPRUS OR UGANDA.

**I**N WESTERN EUROPE, THE WORST OF ANTI-SEMITISM SEEMED OVER. JEWS WERE BUSY, MANY IN AVANT-GARDE THEATER AND MUSIC. <u>ZIONISM DIDN'T SEEM SO IMPORTANT.</u>

**BUT** DEDICATED ZIONISTS WERE NOT WAITING AROUND. THEY WERE PRIVATELY BUYING UP LAND FROM ARAB LANDHOLDERS AND TURNING THEMSELVES INTO FARMERS IN THE HILLS OF PALESTINE.

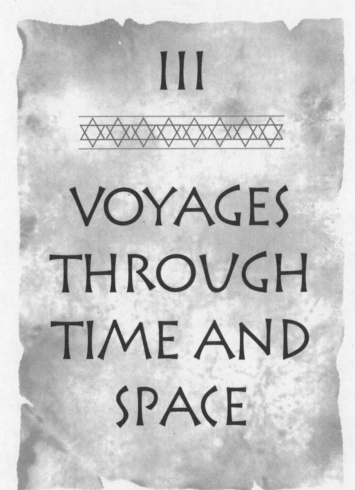

# III

# VOYAGES THROUGH TIME AND SPACE

# 12

# COUSINS ONCE REMOVED

## (PALESTINE–AMERICA)
### 1900–1948

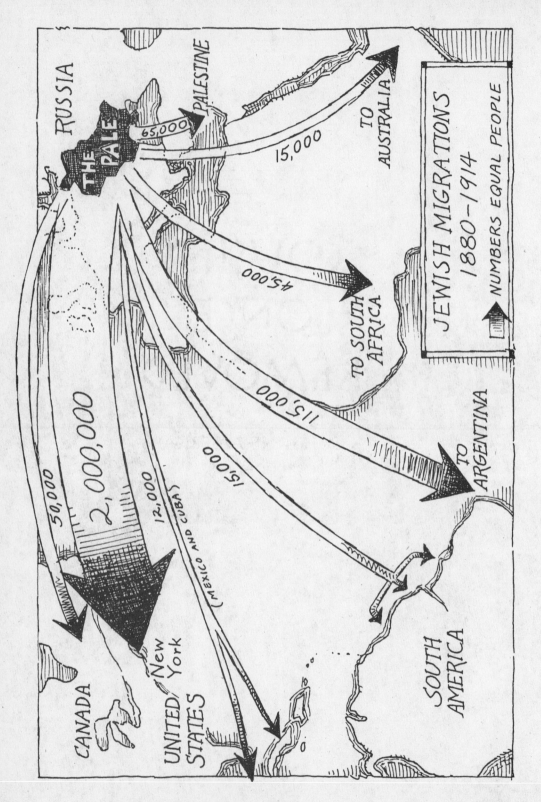

RUSSIA

THE PALE

PALESTINE

65,000

TO AUSTRALIA

15,000

TO SOUTH AFRICA

45,000

115,000

TO ARGENTINA

JEWISH MIGRATIONS
1880–1914
↑ NUMBERS EQUAL PEOPLE

50,000

2,000,000

12,000
(MEXICO AND CUBA)

15,000

CANADA

New York
UNITED STATES

SOUTH AMERICA

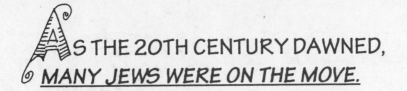

# AS THE 20TH CENTURY DAWNED, MANY JEWS WERE ON THE MOVE.

**A SMALL NUMBER WERE ZIONISTS** SAILING FOR PALESTINE TO BUILD A NEW COUNTRY.

**A FLOOD OF EASTERN EUROPEAN JEWS,** EMBODYING YIDDISH CULTURE, WERE HEADING FOR THE HIGH-SPEED LIFE OF THE UNITED STATES.

**SOME WERE SOCIALISTS** STAYING BEHIND IN EUROPE, TRYING TO CHANGE AND IMPROVE SOCIETY.

# EUROPE

**O**THER JEWS OF WESTERN EUROPE WERE BUSY FITTING IN, MAKING IMPORTANT CONTRIBUTIONS TO BUSINESS, LIBERAL POLITICS, AND CULTURE—ESPECIALLY IN GERMANY.

> GERMANS ARE SO RATIONAL, ETHICAL, AND REASONABLE.

**G**ERMAN JEWS WON NOBEL PRIZES IN THE SCIENCES. A GERMAN-JEWISH WOMAN WAS AN OLYMPIC GOLD MEDALIST IN FENCING. GERMAN AND VIENNESE MUSICIANS OF JEWISH BACKGROUND, LIKE STRAUSS, MAHLER, AND SCHOENBERG, CREATED INNOVATIVE MUSIC.

IN BUSINESS, POLITICS, AND ART, JEWS WERE RISK-TAKERS. FOR THEM, THE INSECURITIES OF THE MODERN WORLD WERE NOTHING NEW.

HEY, AFTER WHAT WE'VE BEEN THROUGH, WHAT'S A LITTLE MORE TRAUMA AND STRESS?

IN THE LATE 1920s, THE JEWS APPEARED TO BE ACCEPTED IN CHRISTIAN SOCIETY. **THEIR INTERMARRIAGE RATE WAS 50%.**

BUT JEWISH PROMINENCE ON THE RIGHT AND LEFT PROVIDED ANTI-SEMITES WITH PLENTY OF AMMUNITION.

BANKING CONSPIRATORS!

CULTURALLY CORRUPT.

COMMUNISTS!

**IN EASTERN EUROPE,** DURING WORLD WAR I, AS RUSSIAN JEWS FOUGHT GERMAN JEWS AT THE FRONT, CZARIST RUSSIA CONTINUED TO LABEL JEWS AS TRAITORS. WHEN THE COMMUNIST REVOLUTION BEGAN, RUSSIAN JEWS WERE HOPEFUL OF CHANGE.

**IN** 1917, LENIN GRABBED POWER IN RUSSIA. HE SET UP A REPRESSIVE, ATHEISTIC DICTATORSHIP AND DESTROYED ALL OPPOSITION. JEWISH LENINISTS AVOIDED ANTI-SEMITIC ATTACKS —FOR A TIME.

**BY** THE END OF THE 1920s, LENIN'S SUCCESSOR, STALIN, WAS KILLING JEWISH COMMUNIST OFFICIALS. ALL THE JEWS OF EASTERN EUROPE WERE CAUGHT IN STALIN'S TRAP.

# PALESTINE

FOR THE ZIONISTS, PALESTINE WAS THE END OF THE LONG DIASPORA. YOUNG PIONEERS FORMED COLLECTIVE UNITS, ROLLED UP THEIR SLEEVES, AND WENT TO WORK SETTLING AND CULTIVATING THE LAND.

AN IMMEDIATE QUESTION WAS, IN WHAT LANGUAGE WOULD THE PIONEERS TALK TO EACH OTHER?

WE'LL USE MY LANGUAGE, FRENCH.

NO, MINE, ENGLISH.

SPANISH?

YIDDISH!

GERMAN.

NOT GERMAN, RUSSIAN.

RUSSIAN? NO WAY.

HOW ABOUT HEBREW?

A GAINST ALL ODDS, AN INSPIRED, DRIVEN RUSSIAN IMMIGRANT, **ELIEZER BEN YEHUDA,** LED A 30-YEAR BATTLE FOR HEBREW. <u>WHERE NO WORDS EXISTED, THEY WERE CREATED FROM OLD ROOTS.</u>

W HEN THE KIDS BEGAN TO USE HEBREW ON THE STREET, THE BATTLE WAS WON. *HEBREW, THE ANCIENT LANGUAGE OF THE JEWS, HAD BECOME A PART OF THE MODERN WORLD.*

DURING WORLD WAR I, TURKEY SIDED WITH GERMANY AND DECLARED ZIONISM **ILLEGAL.** JEWISH SETTLEMENTS, STRUGGLING AGAINST THE HARSH LAND AND ARAB AND TURKISH HOSTILITY, WERE LOSING MOMENTUM.

THEN, IN 1917, GREAT BRITAIN REVIVED ZIONIST HOPES BY DECLARING THAT THEY FAVORED THE ESTABLISHMENT OF **A JEWISH NATIONAL HOME IN PALESTINE.** *IT WAS THE FIRST OFFICIAL RECOGNITION OF THE ZIONIST DREAM.*

THE BALFOUR DECLARATION

OFFICIAL

IT WAS NEVER CLEAR WHY BRITAIN DID IT.

PRESSURE FROM INFLUENTIAL JEWS IN ENGLAND AND THE U.S.

TO KEEP PALESTINE OUT OF FRENCH HANDS.

TO WIN OVER THE JEWISH COMMUNISTS OF RUSSIA.

BUT, IN PALESTINE, BRITAIN WOULD PLAY BOTH SIDES OF THE STREET. WHEN THE ARABS, LED BY AN ENGLISHMAN, LAWRENCE OF ARABIA, REBELLED AGAINST THE TURKS, THE BRITISH REWARDED THE ARABS BY PROMISING THEM PALESTINE, ALSO.

THIS WAS JEWISH LAND THREE THOUSAND YEARS AGO.

ARABS HAVE BEEN HERE SINCE THE 7TH CENTURY.

IN 1917, AS THE TIDE OF WAR TURNED IN FAVOR OF THE ALLIES, GREAT BRITAIN INVADED THE OTTOMAN EMPIRE. SHE DEFEATED TURKEY AND OCCUPIED PALESTINE.

AFTER THE WAR, VICTORIOUS GREAT BRITAIN AND FRANCE CARVED UP THE OLD OTTOMAN EMPIRE, CREATING SYRIA, IRAQ, AND SAUDI ARABIA. BRITAIN GOT AUTHORITY OVER PALESTINE.

PASSING INFORMATION TO THE BRITISH FROM INSIDE TURKISH-HELD PALESTINE WAS A HEROIC JEWISH SPY, SARAH AARONSON.

**A**S ARAB OPPOSITION TO ZIONISM GREW VIOLENT, THE LOCAL BRITISH MILITARY APPEARED TO FAVOR THE ARABS. *(IN 1921, IN AN ATTEMPT TO STABILIZE THE AREA, PRO-ZIONIST WINSTON CHURCHILL SPLIT OFF JORDAN FROM PALESTINE.)*

PALESTINE

TRANSJORDAN

PALESTINE

**D**URING THE 1920s, ZIONIST IMMIGRANTS AND INVESTMENT MONEY POURED INTO PALESTINE. FARMS, FACTORIES, AND SETTLEMENTS MULTIPLIED. AGRICULTURAL AND INDUSTRIAL COLLECTIVES, CALLED

## **KIBBUTZIM,**

CAPTURED THE IMAGINATION OF JEWISH PIONEERS.

*IT WAS A BOOM TIME. IDEALISTS AND HUSTLERS WERE BUYING, BUILDING, AND SPECULATING. THERE WERE AS MANY DEALS AS THERE WERE ROCKS ON THE HILLS OF PALESTINE.*

AS ARAB LANDLORDS SOLD LAND TO JEWS, THE DISPLACED ARAB PEASANTS BEGAN TO COME TOGETHER BEHIND THE IDEA OF ARAB NATIONALISM. THEY TURNED THEIR FRUSTRATION INTO **ATTACKS ON JEWISH SETTLEMENTS.**

WE ARE THE TRUE RULERS OF PALESTINE!

1900 YEARS AGO, JEWISH DEFENDERS OF THEIR HOMELAND HAD LAID DOWN THEIR WEAPONS. NOW THEY PICKED THEM UP AGAIN.

FACED WITH ARAB HOSTILITY AND ENGLISH VACILLATION, THE JEWS FORMED THEIR OWN DEFENSE FORCE CALLED THE

## HAGANAH...

... EVEN AS THEY HARNESSED THE JORDAN RIVER, BUILT SCHOOLS AND CULTURAL CENTERS, AND LINKED THE COUNTRY WITH BUSES.

IN THE '30s, EUROPEAN JEWS, ESCAPING NAZI VIOLENCE, POURED INTO PALESTINE. AT THE SAME TIME, PALESTINIAN ARAB RIOTING AGAINST THE JEWS INCREASED.

THE BRITISH ANSWER WAS TO TRY TO LIMIT JEWISH IMMIGRATION AND RESTRICT HAGANAH ACTIVITIES.

FRUSTRATED BY HAGANAH CAUTION, <u>VLADIMIR JABOTINSKY</u>, MILITANT—AND POETICAL—NATIONALIST, FORMED A GUERRILLA ARMY CALLED THE <u>**IRGUN.**</u> THE IRGUN DEFIED THE BRITISH AND WENT ON THE ATTACK.

THE JEWS OF PALESTINE— ZIONISTS, CAPITALISTS, ORTHODOX, REVISIONISTS— HAD NOW GROWN STRONG ENOUGH TO RUN THEIR OWN COUNTRY—IF THEY EVER GOT THE CHANCE.

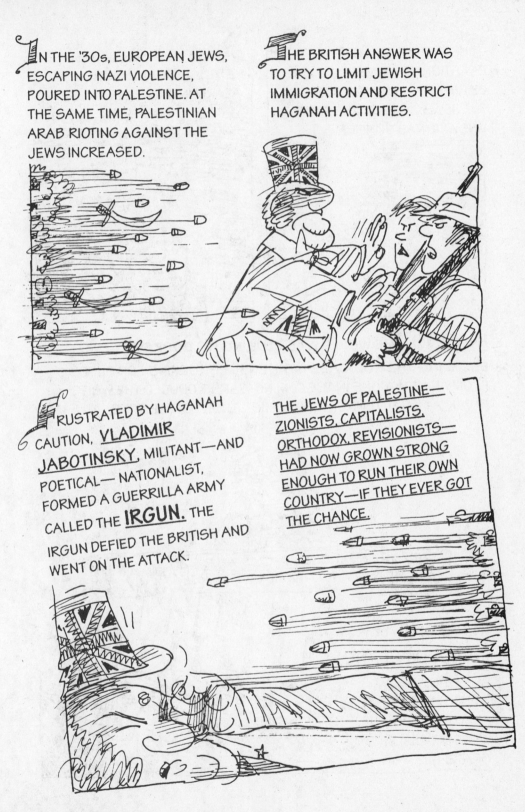

207

THE BRITISH CALLED FOR THE PARTITION OF PALESTINE BETWEEN ARABS AND JEWS. THE JEWS AGREED. THE ARAB ANSWER WAS GUNFIRE.

ARAB VIOLENCE, JEWISH RETALIATION, AND BRITISH ALARM INTENSIFIED.

**IN 1939,** THE WORLD WAS CLOSING ITS DOORS TO JEWS ESCAPING THE HOLOCAUST. THE ENGLISH, LOOKING FOR SUPPORT FROM ARAB NATIONS IN THE COMING WAR, PRODUCED THE WHITE PAPER, A PLAN TO END JEWISH IMMIGRATION TO PALESTINE.

PALESTINE
JEWS NO LONGER WELCOME

**IN 1939, HITLER INVADED POLAND.**

PALESTINIAN JEWS JOINED THE BRITISH ARMY. THE BRITISH WERE OFFICIALLY GRATEFUL.

**B**UT, THROUGHOUT THE WAR, BRITISH POLICY NEVER CHANGED. WHEN BOATLOADS OF JEWS FLEEING HITLER ARRIVED IN PALESTINE, **THE BRITISH DENIED THEM ENTRY.**

KEEP O

NO JEWS ALLOWED

**T**HE JEWS OF PALESTINE SET UP A SMUGGLING OPERATION IN EUROPE. USING ANY FLOATABLE TUB, THEY SNEAKED REFUGEES PAST THE ENGLISH BLOCKADE.

SPLASH

SHHH

**P**ALESTINIAN JEWS, WHO HAD THEMSELVES ESCAPED RUSSIAN POGROMS, WATCHED IN HORROR AS FELLOW JEWS WERE FORCED BACK TO A EUROPEAN HELL.

SOB S...

NO JEW

NO

**A**FTER THE WAR, THE OLD BRITISH POLICIES CONTINUED, **AND THE JEWS WENT ON THE ATTACK.** IN '46, THE IRGUN BLEW UP BRITISH HEADQUARTERS AT THE KING DAVID HOTEL IN JERUSALEM.

**T**HE BRITISH RETALIATED BY HANGING JEWISH FIGHTERS. BUT, WITH EVERY BRITISH ACTION, THE JEWS HIT BACK HARDER.

**I**N 1947, THE BRITISH GAVE UP AND TOSSED THE PROBLEM TO THE UNITED NATIONS.

THE ARABS WILL DESTROY THAT BUNCH OF GUNMEN AND THAT'LL BE THAT!

IN THE U.N., AN ODD COUPLE, THE U.S. AND RUSSIA, HAD REASON TO SUPPORT A JEWISH STATE.

THE JEWISH VOTE IN THE NEXT ELECTION.

A SOCIALIST STATE IN THE MIDDLE EAST.

THE U.N. VOTED TO DIVIDE PALESTINE BETWEEN ARABS AND JEWS. THE JEWS ACCEPTED IT. THE ARABS REJECTED IT. *THE SURROUNDING ARAB STATES READIED FOR WAR AGAINST THE JEWS.*

IN MAY 1948 THE STATE OF ISRAEL WAS BORN IN THE LAND OF ABRAHAM AND SARAH. *THE JEWS PREPARED TO DEFEND IT.*

# THE UNITED STATES

THE JEWS WHO LEFT EASTERN EUROPE AT THE TURN OF THE CENTURY SHARED ONE TRAIT, THE WILLINGNESS TO RISK THE UNKNOWN FOR A DREAM. **THEY HUGGED RELATIVES, TRAVELED BY NIGHT, AND MADE THEIR WAY ACROSS A DANGEROUS EUROPE.**

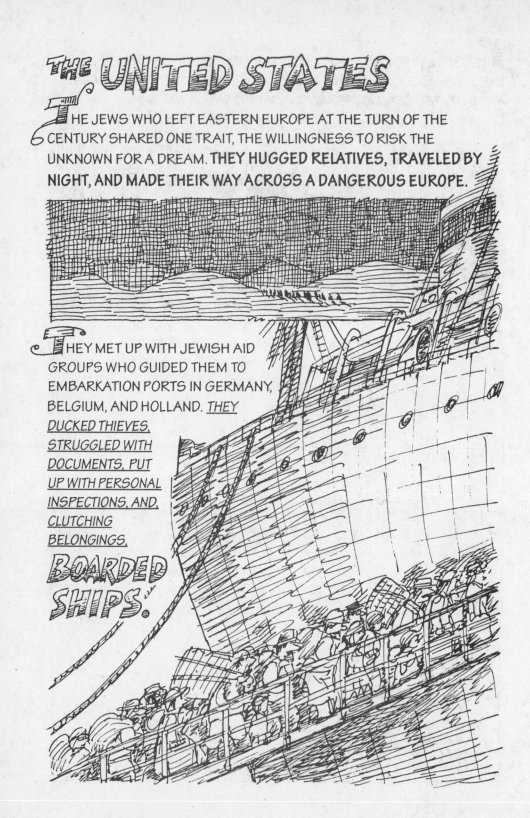

THEY MET UP WITH JEWISH AID GROUPS WHO GUIDED THEM TO EMBARKATION PORTS IN GERMANY, BELGIUM, AND HOLLAND. _THEY DUCKED THIEVES, STRUGGLED WITH DOCUMENTS, PUT UP WITH PERSONAL INSPECTIONS, AND, CLUTCHING BELONGINGS,_ BOARDED SHIPS.

CROWDED INTO STEERAGE, SICK, NOSTALGIC, AND EXCITED, THEY HEADED FOR ENGLAND, AUSTRALIA, SOUTH AFRICA, SOUTH AMERICA, CANADA, **AND, ESPECIALLY, THE UNITED STATES.**

THEY'D HEARD THAT THE U.S. WAS A MAGICAL LAND WHERE THE STREETS WERE PAVED WITH GOLD.

EQUALITY. RICHES. NON-KOSHER FOOD.

EMMA LAZARUS, A NEW YORK–BORN JEWISH POET, WROTE THE WORDS THAT APPEAR ON THE STATUE OF LIBERTY IN NEW YORK HARBOR.

GIVE ME YOUR TIRED, YOUR POOR, YOUR HUDDLED MASSES...

As we have seen, the Sephardim arrived in South America in the 1500s. When the Inquisition showed up, they moved north to the Dutch and English colonies.

In the mid-1800s, German Jews arrived in the U.S. with their business skills and Reform Judaism. They quickly found success as merchants.

Now, the shtetl Jews jammed Ellis Island, gateway to New York, terrified they might be sent back to Europe.

AS THESE FOREIGN-LOOKING, CLAMOROUS JEWS STRUGGLED DOWN THE GANGPLANKS ONTO MANHATTAN ISLAND, THE AFFLUENT, UPTOWN GERMAN JEWS WATCHED *IN EMBARRASSMENT.*

UGH. WHAT WOULD THE GENTILES SAY IF THEY KNEW WE WERE RELATED TO SUCH PEOPLE?

YET, IN DIASPORA TRADITION, THEY DID COME DOWNTOWN AND ESTABLISH SUPPORT SERVICES FOR THEIR POOR COUSINS.

THE NEWCOMERS CRAMMED INTO THE FIRETRAP TENEMENTS OF THE LOWER EAST SIDE. THEY FILLED ITS NARROW STREETS WITH CARTS, HORSES, NOISE, GARBAGE, AND HOLE-IN-THE-WALL SHOPS AND SYNAGOGUES—*A CHURNING WORLD OF IMMIGRANT ENERGY.*

COATS
HATS
GLOVES
SHOES
BAKERY
WURST
LUNCH
SALE 25¢

THE SEWING MACHINE AND A GROWING CONSUMER POPULATION CREATED A HUGE NEED FOR CHEAP LABOR. THE POOR JEWISH MEN, WOMEN, AND CHILDREN WERE DRAWN INTO THE DEADLY WORLD OF THE NEW YORK *GARMENT SWEATSHOPS.*

TO AVOID THE SWEATSHOPS, SOME JEWS WOULD COMPETE FOR PENNIES, BUYING AND SELLING ANYTHING.

SHARPEST PENCILS!

TASTIEST PICKLES!

STRONGEST SHOELACES!

*MEANWHILE, SOCIAL WORKERS, YIDDISH NEWSPAPERS, THE YIDDISH THEATER, AND PUBLIC SCHOOLS WERE HELPING THE JEWS MOVE INTO THE BIG, OUTSIDE WORLD, DESPITE THE PROTESTS OF THEIR RABBIS.*

**SOME FOUND THEIR FAITH IN THE LABOR MOVEMENT.** THEY CONFRONTED THE BOSSES AND HELPED WIN ENORMOUS IMPROVEMENTS IN THE WORKING CONDITIONS OF THE GARMENT TRADES.

WE HAVE THE POWER OF PRODUCTION

UNION FOR AND OF THE WORKERS

ORGANI...

OTHERS LEARNED TO ADAPT TO THE SYSTEM AND BECAME **RICH.**

MY BOY, STAY AWAY FROM CIGARS AND BUTCHERING.

THE REAL MONEY IS IN REAL ESTATE, JUNK, AND...

...ENTERTAINMENT. PENNY ARCADES ARE CHEAP TO RENT.

THE IMMIGRANTS LABORED LONG HOURS TO SEND THEIR CHILDREN TO COLLEGE TO BECOME **REAL AMERICANS.**

LIFE HERE MAY BE ROUGH...

?

?

...BUT IT SURE BEATS THE UKRAINE.

ODERN BRIDGES, TUNNELS, AND SUBWAYS APPEARED AT THE SAME TIME AS THE IMMIGRANTS. THE JEWS USED THEM TO MOVE TO BROOKLYN, THE BRONX, THE SUBURBS, AND OTHER CITIES— _TO HOMES WITH LAWNS AND PRIVATE BATHROOMS._

**D**URING THE
FIRST WORLD
WAR, PATRIOT AND
ANTIFOREIGN
GROUPS PUSHED
FOR LIMITATIONS
ON IMMIGRATION.
THEY FEARED
COMMUNISTS AND
THE POISONING OF
THEIR CULTURE.

WE MUST STOP
THEM FROM
TURNING US INTO
A DARK-SKINNED...

... ITALIAN, SLAVIC,
CATHOLIC, JEWISH,
COMMUNIST, ASIAN
COUNTRY!

**B**Y 1924, THE U.S. HAD CLOSED THE DOOR ON EASTERN EUROPEAN
IMMIGRATION. _IN THE '30s, AS THE NAZI MENACE GREW_, THIS POLICY
WOULD PREVENT EUROPEAN JEWS FROM ESCAPING TO THE U.S.

IN THE U.S., THE CHILDREN OF THE IMMIGRANTS LEFT BEHIND THE ORTHODOXY OF THEIR PARENTS AND CUSTOMIZED A JUDAISM THAT WOULD FIT *THEIR NEW LIFESTYLE.*

THIS FIRST GENERATION MOVED INTO TRADITIONAL PROFESSIONS LIKE LAW AND MEDICINE. BUT IT ALSO PLAYED A DOMINANT ROLE IN THE CREATION OF *TIN PAN ALLEY, THE AMERICAN MUSICAL THEATER,* AND *THE HOLLYWOOD MOVIE INDUSTRY.*

THESE DARING CHILDREN OF EX-SHTETL PEDDLERS PUT TOGETHER THE EARLY FILM STUDIOS AND GLITTERING ENTERTAINMENT PALACES THAT GAVE BIRTH TO THE SPECTACULAR **AMERICAN MOTION PICTURE.**

PARADISE ALHAMBRA GRANDE

COMING FEATURE
EPIC
STARS

THE PUBLIC IS NEVER WRONG.

I CONVERTED. I USED TO BE JEWISH, NOW I'M INCORRIGIBLE.

JEWISH COMICS CREATED A WHOLE NEW KIND OF AMERICAN HUMOR—SELF-MOCKING, SUBVERSIVE, AND ABSURDIST.

LAND THAT I LOVE...

IRVING BERLIN, BORN IN SIBERIA, WROTE "GOD BLESS AMERICA," "EASTER PARADE," AND "WHITE CHRISTMAS."

THE LATEST NEWS, LIVE FROM OUR STUDIOS!

JEWS WERE INFLUENTIAL IN THE NEWSPAPER BUSINESS AND IN EARLY RADIO AND TELEVISION.

IN THE 1930s, ALONG WITH MANY SUCCESSES, JEWS CONTINUED TO RUN INTO QUOTAS IN SOME SCHOOLS AND BUSINESSES.

NO JEWS

NO JEWS  NO JEWS  NO JEWS  NO

PERSONNEL

IN THE DEPTHS OF THE GREAT DEPRESSION, SOME DISAFFECTED JEWS WERE ATTRACTED TO A COMMUNIST (AND ANTIFASCIST) IDEAL. BUT PRESIDENT ROOSEVELT PULLED THEM BACK WITH HIS SOCIAL WELFARE PROGRAMS.

A NEW DEAL FOR AMERICA

HELP WANTED

JEWS WELCOME

CONFIRMATION OF MASS MURDER OF JEWS

JEWS FOUND A WELCOME IN HIS ADMINISTRATION, BUT, AS THE U.S. ENTERED THE **SECOND WORLD WAR,** ROOSEVELT HELD BACK FROM TAKING SPECIAL STEPS TO SAVE JEWS TRAPPED BY THE NAZIS.

DURING WORLD WAR II, INDIVIDUAL AMERICAN JEWS DID WHAT THEY COULD TO HELP EUROPEAN JEWRY, BUT, IN LATER YEARS, THEY WOULD ASK THEMSELVES HOW THEY MIGHT HAVE DONE MORE.

WAR NEWS

ATROCITIES AGAINST JEWS REPORTED

LATEST MODELS FROM DETROIT

JEWISH AGENCIES FOUGHT HARD TO GET EUROPEAN JEWS INTO THE U.S., BUT, BECAUSE OF U.S. GOVERNMENT POLICIES, THOSE WHO GOT OUT WERE OFTEN LEFT TO WANDER THE WORLD *IN SEARCH OF SAFETY.*

INFLUENTIAL JEWS DID MANAGE TO BRING IN GERMAN JEWISH SCHOLARS AND SCIENTISTS WHO WOULD GREATLY AID THE ALLIED WAR EFFORT AND ENRICH THE UNITED STATES.

# 13

## CATACLYSM

### (THE HOLOCAUST)
### 1918–1946

WARLIKE, SELF-CONFIDENT GERMANY AT THE START OF WORLD WAR I.

GERMANY IN 1918, AT THE END OF THE WAR, DEFEATED AND ECONOMICALLY SHACKLED BY FRANCE, ENGLAND, AND THE U.S.

THE GERMAN WEIMAR REPUBLIC, BORN IN 1919 — DEMOCRATIC, LIBERAL, WEAK ooo

ooo AND HATED BY BITTER GERMAN EX-ARMY OFFICERS, INDUSTRIALISTS, AND THE PRUSSIAN OLD GUARD.

IN THE 1920s, WEIMAR GLITTERED WITH AN AVANT-GARDE ARTISTIC AND LITERARY CULTURE, AND THE JEWS WERE IN THE CENTER OF THE ACTION. ON THE SURFACE, IT WAS AN EXUBERANT, PASSIONATE TIME.

BUT COMMUNISM, INFLATION, AND UNEMPLOYMENT WERE SPREADING ACROSS EUROPE. _THE GERMAN RIGHT ACCUSED THE COMMUNISTS AND JEWS OF CORRUPTING GERMAN CULTURE._

JEWS!

COMMUNISTS!

BOTH OF THEM!

MANY GERMAN JEWS EXCUSED THE RIGHT-WING EXTREMISTS.

THIS HAS NOTHING TO DO WITH US. I WAS EVEN DECORATED FOR BRAVERY IN THE ARMY. IT'LL PASS.

IN 1923, IN MUNICH, THERE APPEARED A FRINGE POLITICAL GROUP CALLED THE NATIONAL SOCIALISTS—**THE NAZIS**—LED BY AN EX-GERMAN CORPORAL, ADOLF HITLER

ADOLF HAD A MAD DREAM OF GERMAN WORLD DOMINATION ● ● ●

● ● ● AND AN IRRATIONAL HATRED OF THE JEWS.

HITLER WAS A SPELLBINDING SPEAKER. HE PROMISED VIOLENCE AGAINST THE JEWS, AND MANY SUFFERING GERMANS SUPPORTED HIM.

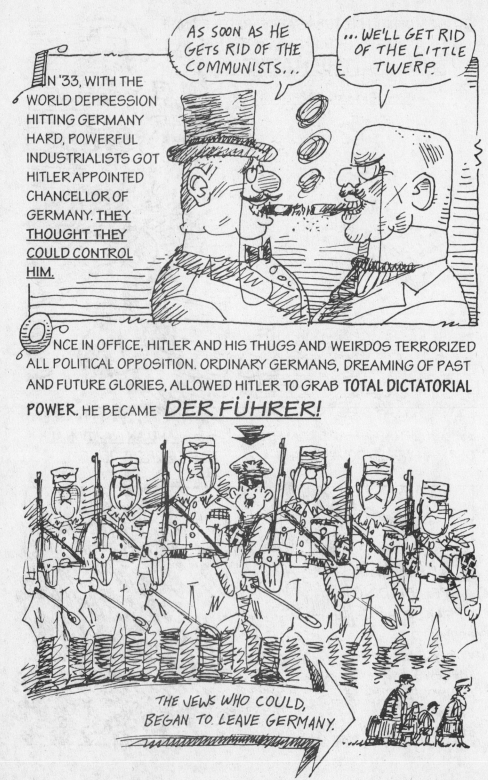

IN '33, WITH THE WORLD DEPRESSION HITTING GERMANY HARD, POWERFUL INDUSTRIALISTS GOT HITLER APPOINTED CHANCELLOR OF GERMANY. <u>THEY THOUGHT THEY COULD CONTROL HIM.</u>

AS SOON AS HE GETS RID OF THE COMMUNISTS...

...WE'LL GET RID OF THE LITTLE TWERP.

ONCE IN OFFICE, HITLER AND HIS THUGS AND WEIRDOS TERRORIZED ALL POLITICAL OPPOSITION. ORDINARY GERMANS, DREAMING OF PAST AND FUTURE GLORIES, ALLOWED HITLER TO GRAB **TOTAL DICTATORIAL POWER.** HE BECAME _**DER FÜHRER!**_

THE JEWS WHO COULD, BEGAN TO LEAVE GERMANY.

GERMAN SCHOLARS, CLERGY, STUDENTS, AND SCIENTISTS SWALLOWED HITLER'S BIZARRE FANTASY THAT INFERIOR RACES WERE OUT TO SEXUALLY INFECT THE GERMAN MASTER RACE.

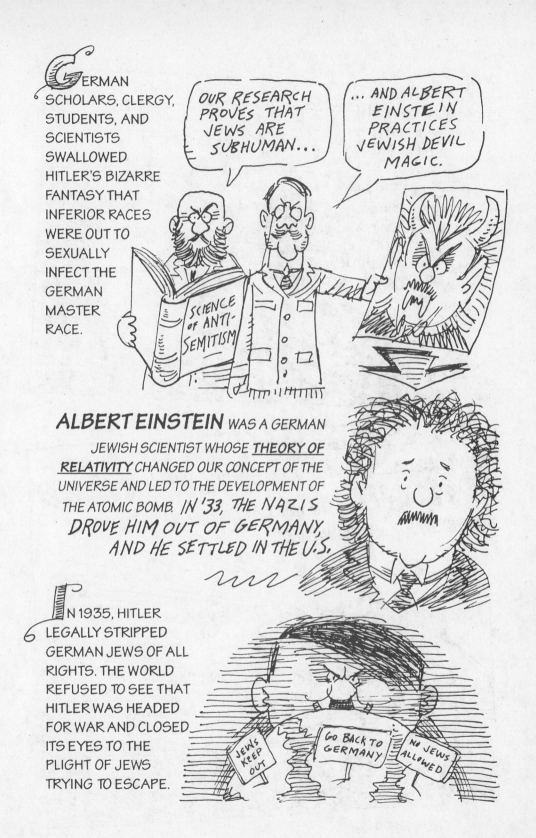

OUR RESEARCH PROVES THAT JEWS ARE SUBHUMAN...

...AND ALBERT EINSTEIN PRACTICES JEWISH DEVIL MAGIC.

SCIENCE OF ANTI-SEMITISM

**ALBERT EINSTEIN** WAS A GERMAN JEWISH SCIENTIST WHOSE **THEORY OF RELATIVITY** CHANGED OUR CONCEPT OF THE UNIVERSE AND LED TO THE DEVELOPMENT OF THE ATOMIC BOMB. *IN '33, THE NAZIS DROVE HIM OUT OF GERMANY, AND HE SETTLED IN THE U.S.*

IN 1935, HITLER LEGALLY STRIPPED GERMAN JEWS OF ALL RIGHTS. THE WORLD REFUSED TO SEE THAT HITLER WAS HEADED FOR WAR AND CLOSED ITS EYES TO THE PLIGHT OF JEWS TRYING TO ESCAPE.

JEWS KEEP OUT

GO BACK TO GERMANY

NO JEWS ALLOWED

IN 1938, HITLER ESCALATED HIS ANTI-JEWISH VIOLENCE: DESTROYING AND STEALING PROPERTY, BEATING AND RAPING JEWS, HOLDING THEM AS HOSTAGES, AND FORCING THEM INTO SLAVE LABOR CAMPS.

THE JEWS, NOW PAUPERS, WERE STILL TRYING TO ESCAPE, BUT MANY REMAINED TRAPPED. THEN, IN 1939, HITLER INVADED POLAND. THE WAR WAS ON, AND ALL OF EUROPEAN JEWRY WAS IN MORTAL DANGER.

IN 1941, GERMANY INVADED RUSSIA. GERMAN DEATH SQUADS, JOINED BY LITHUANIAN AND UKRAINIAN COLLABORATORS, SLAUGHTERED JEWS. *THE GREAT EASTERN EUROPEAN JEWISH TRADITION LAY DYING IN MASS GRAVES.*

HITLER BEGAN CARRYING OUT THE **FINAL SOLUTION** TO THE JEWISH QUESTION—WITH THE HELP OF GERMAN TECHNICIANS.

HE SAYS HE NEEDS BIG, EFFICIENT GAS CHAMBERS AND OVENS.

FROM 1942 TO 1945, THE NAZIS KILLED STAGGERING NUMBERS OF JEWS IN **EXTERMINATION CAMPS** LIKE **AUSCHWITZ** AND **TREBLINKA** IN POLAND, AND **DACHAU** IN GERMANY. BY WAR'S END, THERE WERE THOUSANDS OF CAMPS.

As they transported Jews to the camps, the Germans used every trick to disguise the destination.

FAKE POSTCARDS TELLING OF GOOD TIMES IN THE CAMPS.

GREETINGS FROM BAVARIA

OFFICIAL WORK PERMITS PROMISING FUTURE JOBS.

PASSPORT

CAMP PHOTOS OF OLD FRIENDS SMILING FOR THE CAMERA.

PICTURES OF HEALTHY PEOPLE ENTERING SHOWER ROOMS.

POOL SHOWERS

After a while, the Jews could no longer be deceived.

235

THE NAZIS KEPT THE JEWS DEMORALIZED. <u>AT ANY SIGN OF PROTEST, THEY WOULD ATTACK THE MOST VULNERABLE.</u> THEY'D GRAB A BABY FROM THE MOTHER'S ARMS, SMASH THE CHILD AGAINST A WALL, AND HAND THE REMAINS BACK TO THE MOTHER.

IN THE CAMPS, THE JEWS HELD ON TO THEIR SANITY BY MAINTAINING THEIR CULTURE IN THE MIDDLE OF THE BARBARITY. THEY PUT ON CONCERTS AND LECTURES, AND STUDIED THEIR HISTORY AND FAITH. **THEY WERE A FLAME THAT WOULD NOT DIE.**

MANY OF THE COUNTRIES OF THE WORLD CHOSE NOT TO HEAR THE RUMORS OF THE **FINAL SOLUTION** AND KEPT THEIR DOORS CLOSED TO JEWS ON THE RUN.

BUT A FEW COUNTRIES AND INDIVIDUALS TOOK RISKS AND AIDED ESCAPEES.

I TELL YOU, THERE ARE NO JEWS HERE.

REVOLT WAS ALMOST IMPOSSIBLE, BUT MANY JEWS FOUGHT BACK WHEREVER AND HOWEVER THEY COULD.

JEWS MADE LAST-DITCH STANDS IN EXTERMINATION CENTERS.

ESCAPED JEWS BECAME GUERRILLA FIGHTERS WITH THE PARTISANS OF EASTERN EUROPE.

THE INCREDIBLE JEWISH UPRISING OF THE WARSAW GHETTO SHOOK GERMAN CONFIDENCE.

JEWS FOUGHT IN THE FRENCH RESISTANCE.

JEWS FOUGHT IN EVERY ALLIED ARMY.

HEROIC WOMEN FOUGHT IN THE UNDERGROUND. HANNAH SENESH PARACHUTED INTO EUROPE TO HELP ESCAPEES. CHAIKA GROSSMAN LED GHETTO UPRISINGS IN POLAND.

IN EVERY GHETTO, JEWS RECORDED THE DETAILS OF THEIR NIGHTMARE IN LETTERS AND DIARIES, SO THE TRUTH WOULD NOT BE LOST.

239

IN 1945, THE GERMAN REICH SURRENDERED AND HITLER KILLED HIMSELF. BY THAT TIME, **THE NAZIS HAD MURDERED 11 MILLION PEOPLE. SIX MILLION OF THEM WERE JEWS. 1.5 MILLION OF THE JEWS WERE CHILDREN.**

SURVIVORS OF THE CAMPS WERE GATHERED IN **DISPLACED PERSONS' CAMPS.** INCREDIBLY, ANTI-SEMITISM STILL LIVED IN CENTRAL EUROPE. THE JEWS NEEDED TO FIND NEW PLACES TO RESTART THEIR LIVES.

EUROPE
PALESTINE
U.S.A.
CANADA
LATIN AMERICA
AUSTRALIA
SOUTH AFRICA

IN 1946, JEWISH AGENTS BEGAN TO HUNT DOWN NAZI WAR CRIMINALS AND BRING THEM TO TRIAL, *AND THE SURVIVORS DEPARTED THE LAND THAT HAD BEEN THE BIRTHPLACE FOR SO MUCH JEWISH ACHIEVEMENT OVER THE CENTURIES.*

# 14

# ARE WE THERE YET?

## (ISRAEL–UNITED STATES)
## 1945–PRESENT

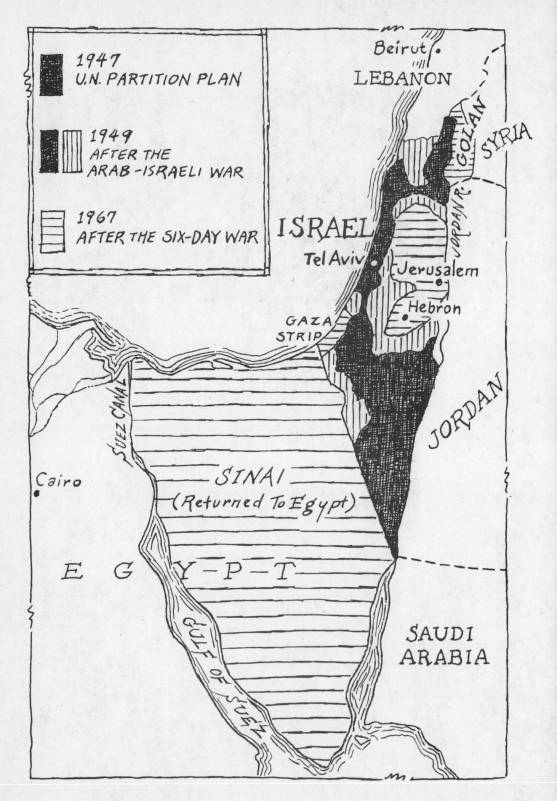

1947
U.N. PARTITION PLAN

1949
AFTER THE
ARAB-ISRAELI WAR

1967
AFTER THE SIX-DAY WAR

Beirut
LEBANON

GOLAN

SYRIA

ISRAEL

Tel Aviv

Jerusalem

Hebron

JORDAN R.

GAZA
STRIP

JORDAN

SUEZ CANAL

Cairo

SINAI
(Returned To Egypt)

E  G  Y - P - T

GULF OF SUEZ

SAUDI
ARABIA

# ISRAEL

IN MAY 1948 ISRAEL, LED BY HER FIRST PRIME MINISTER, **DAVID BEN-GURION,** ASSERTED JEWISH RIGHT TO THE LAND BY BEATING BACK AN ALL-OUT ATTACK FROM THE ARAB STATES.

THE STATE OF ISRAEL HAS ARISEN!

JEWS FROM EVERY PART OF EUROPE, ASIA, AND AFRICA BEGAN TO POUR INTO ISRAEL—INCLUDING THE <u>SEPHARDIM,</u> DRIVEN OUT OF ARAB COUNTRIES AFTER CENTURIES OF LIFE UNDER ISLAMIC RULE.

PALESTINIAN ARABS, PRESSURED BY BOTH JEWISH AND ARAB MILITARY TO LEAVE THEIR HOMES, FOUND LITTLE WELCOME IN NEARBY ARAB STATES.

IN THE '50s, EAST-WEST COLD-WAR SUPERPOWER INTRIGUES INTENSIFIED IN THE REGION. *BACKED BY RUSSIAN ARMS, EGYPT BLOCKADED ISRAELI SHIPPING AND NATIONALIZED THE SUEZ CANAL.*

SUEZ CANAL

ENGLAND AND FRANCE JOINED ISRAEL TO STRIKE AT EGYPT. ISRAEL CAPTURED THE SINAI DESERT AND THE GAZA STRIP.

POW

SUEZ CANAL

THE U.S., WITH A NERVOUS EYE ON RUSSIAN ATOMIC POWER, PRESSURED ISRAEL TO GIVE BACK WHAT SHE'D JUST WON.

DON'T WORRY, THE U.N. WILL GUARD YOUR SECURITY.

IN '67, EGYPT AGAIN BLOCKADED ISRAELI SHIPPING, MASSED ITS ARMY IN THE SINAI, AND GOT THE U.N. TROOPS TO LEAVE. *ISRAEL RETALIATED WITH BOLD AIR STRIKES THAT DESTROYED THE ENTIRE EGYPTIAN AIR FORCE ON THE GROUND.*

THIS IS NOT GOOD. BETTER TO REPORT THAT WE WON.

← EGYPTIAN COMMAND

MISLED BY REPORTS OF EGYPTIAN CONQUEST, JORDANIAN AND SYRIAN TROOPS ATTACKED ISRAEL. ISRAEL HIT BACK.

AT THE END OF WHAT BECAME KNOWN AS THE **SIX-DAY WAR,** A VICTORIOUS ISRAEL HAD GROWN TO INCLUDE *THE WEST BANK OF THE JORDAN RIVER, THE GAZA STRIP, THE SINAI, THE GOLAN HEIGHTS,* AND *THE OLD CITY OF JERUSALEM.*

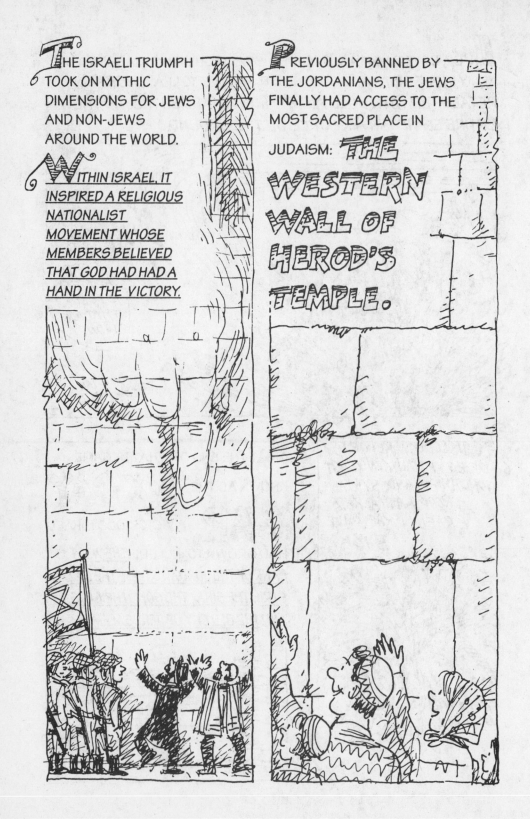

THE ISRAELI TRIUMPH TOOK ON MYTHIC DIMENSIONS FOR JEWS AND NON-JEWS AROUND THE WORLD.

WITHIN ISRAEL, IT INSPIRED A RELIGIOUS NATIONALIST MOVEMENT WHOSE MEMBERS BELIEVED THAT GOD HAD HAD A HAND IN THE VICTORY.

PREVIOUSLY BANNED BY THE JORDANIANS, THE JEWS FINALLY HAD ACCESS TO THE MOST SACRED PLACE IN JUDAISM: *THE WESTERN WALL OF HEROD'S TEMPLE.*

IN 1973, STEEL-WILLED, GRANDMOTHERLY ISRAELI PRIME MINISTER **GOLDA MEIR** WAS CAUGHT OFF GUARD BY A SYRIAN AND EGYPTIAN SURPRISE ATTACK.

WE MUST GUARD AGAINST OVER-CONFIDENCE, UH-OH!

GOLDA STRUCK BACK HARD. ISRAEL DROVE SOUTH ACROSS THE SUEZ CANAL AND NORTH TO TAKE MORE OF THE GOLAN.

PLAYING BOTH SIDES, U.S. PRESIDENT **NIXON** GOT ISRAEL AND EGYPT TO AGREE TO A LAND-FOR-PEACE PACT.

IF YOU GIVE BACK A LITTLE LAND NOW, THE WORLD WILL LIKE YOU BETTER.

IF YOU LET THEM KEEP SOME OF THE LAND NOW, YOU'LL GET IT ALL LATER.

IN 1978, PRESIDENT **SADAT** OF EGYPT BROKE WITH OTHER ARAB STATES TO TRADE RECOGNITION OF ISRAEL FOR THE RETURN OF THE SINAI. IN '81, SADAT WAS KILLED BY ARAB ASSASSINS.

Uring this period, as Israel continued to expand into Palestinian communities in the West Bank ...

...The Arab nations used the world's thirst for oil as pressure to try to isolate Israel...

...And they backed the guerrilla activities of the **Palestine <u>Liberation Organization</u>,** led by Yasir Arafat.

No peace, no recognition, no negotiation with the Jews.

EGALITARIANISM FIRST!

THE LAW OF MOSES FIRST!

PEACE FIRST!

SECURITY FIRST!

CAPITALISM FIRST!

DEFINE A JEW FIRST!

Meanwhile, in Israel, **the only democracy in the middle east,** the liberal <u>Labor Party</u>, whose values had built the Jewish state, faced the growing strength of the more traditional and hawkish <u>Likud Party.</u>

IN THE '80s, P.L.O. HOSTILITY INCREASED AND YOUNG WEST BANK PALESTINIANS RIOTED. *ISRAEL'S RESPONSE WAS TOUGH AND BLOODY. JEWS OUTSIDE AND INSIDE ISRAEL BEGAN TO QUESTION HARSH ISRAELI METHODS.*

IN '92, **YITZHAK RABIN,** AN ISRAELI MILITARY HERO, BECAME PRIME MINISTER AND SPARKED TALK OF A LAND–FOR–PEACE INITIATIVE.

I KNOW SOMEONE WHO KNOWS SOMEONE.

I CAN GET TO SOMEONE WHO'D BE WILLING TO TALK TO SOMEONE.

MEETINGS BETWEEN JEWS AND PALESTINIANS IN OSLO, NORWAY, PRODUCED, IN 1993, A **PEACE ACCORD** THAT INCLUDED A SCHEDULE FOR ISRAELI WITHDRAWAL FROM PARTS OF THE WEST BANK. *THE REACTIONS WERE PREDICTABLE.*

YOU RECOGNIZE US, WE'LL RECOGNIZE YOU.

TOO VAGUE.

TOO CLEAR.

WONDERFUL.

A DISASTER.

251

ALONG WITH THE PEACE PLAN, <u>THE ISRAELI ECONOMY BOOMED, AND GREAT NUMBERS OF RUSSIAN IMMIGRANTS ARRIVED.</u> ETHIOPIAN JEWS WERE ALSO BROUGHT IN THROUGH A GUTSY ISRAELI AIR RESCUE.

ELVIS HUMMUS & PIZZA

THE PEACE PLAN HAS BROUGHT ROCK CONCERTS, FROZEN YOGURT, AND CABLE TV.

GOD DOES NOT APPROVE.

ISRAELI, JORDANIAN, AND PALESTINIAN TOURIST BUREAUS MADE PLANS.

THE DEAD SEA WILL MAKE A GREAT AMUSEMENT PARK.

WE'LL ADVERTISE THE LOWEST RIDES ON EARTH.

THE TRUCE HELD, DESPITE EXTREMISTS ON BOTH SIDES ATTEMPTING TO SABOTAGE IT. **THEN A TWENTY-FIVE-YEAR-OLD ISRAELI RELIGIOUS FANATIC KILLED RABIN.**

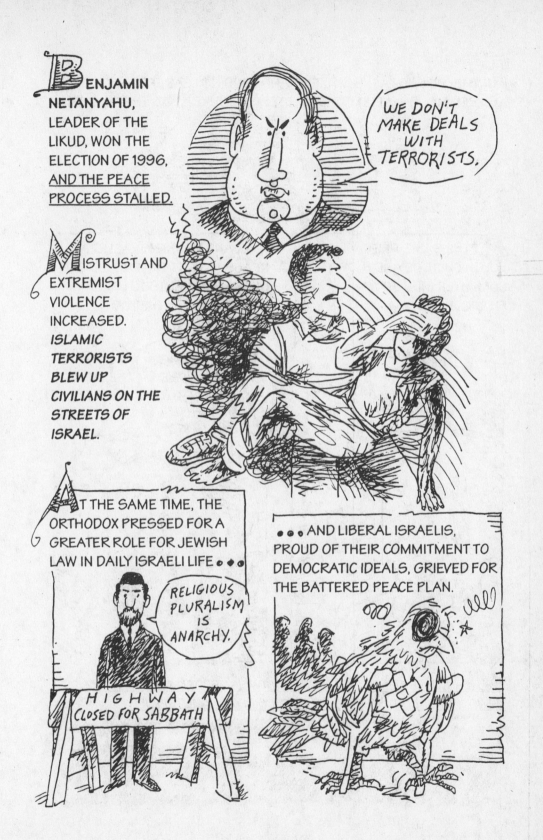

**B**ENJAMIN NETANYAHU, LEADER OF THE LIKUD, WON THE ELECTION OF 1996, <u>AND THE PEACE PROCESS STALLED.</u>

WE DON'T MAKE DEALS WITH TERRORISTS.

**M**ISTRUST AND EXTREMIST VIOLENCE INCREASED. *ISLAMIC TERRORISTS BLEW UP CIVILIANS ON THE STREETS OF ISRAEL.*

**A**T THE SAME TIME, THE ORTHODOX PRESSED FOR A GREATER ROLE FOR JEWISH LAW IN DAILY ISRAELI LIFE...

RELIGIOUS PLURALISM IS ANARCHY.

HIGHWAY CLOSED FOR SABBATH

...AND LIBERAL ISRAELIS, PROUD OF THEIR COMMITMENT TO DEMOCRATIC IDEALS, GRIEVED FOR THE BATTERED PEACE PLAN.

IN THE '90s, ISRAEL'S CITIZENS AND FEUDING LEADERS —POLITICAL AND RELIGIOUS—ATTEMPTED TO STEER A COURSE INTO THE FUTURE.

AT THE SAME TIME, A YOUTH CULTURE AND HIGH-TECH COMPUTER INDUSTRY FLOURISHED . . .

SO ARE WE ALL GOING OUT FOR A CAFE LATTE AT THE INTERNET CAFE AFTER WORK?

. . . AND YOUNG ISRAELIS REACHED PAST THE PREJUDICES OF THEIR PARENTS TO OFFER HOPE THROUGH THEIR ART, MUSIC, AND POLITICAL SATIRE.

THE GOVERNMENT HAS ACCUSED US OF LACKING TASTE AND CREATIVITY.

WE MUST BE DOING SOMETHING RIGHT.

OFFICIAL

MEANWHILE, DESPITE CONFLICTS BETWEEN ISRAELI AND DIASPORA JEWS, ISRAEL CONTINUED TO BE A BEACON FOR WORLD JEWRY.

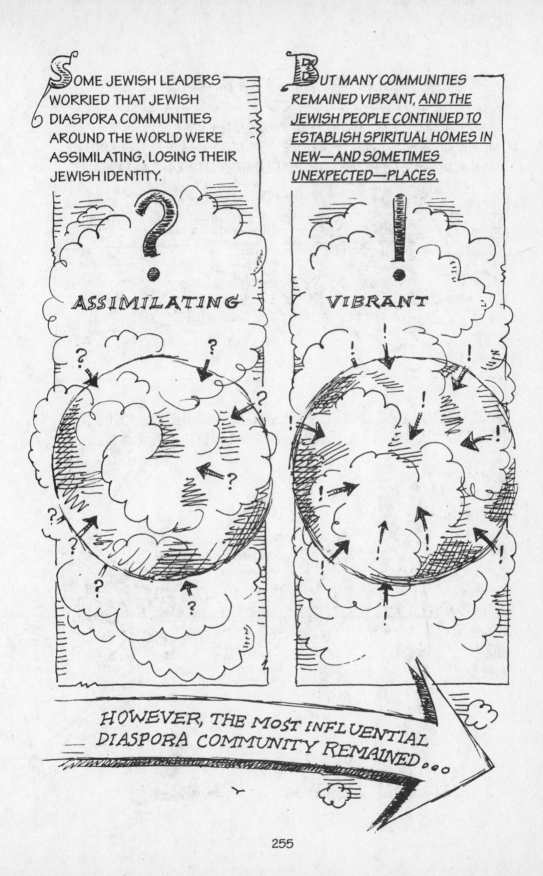

**S**OME JEWISH LEADERS WORRIED THAT JEWISH DIASPORA COMMUNITIES AROUND THE WORLD WERE ASSIMILATING, LOSING THEIR JEWISH IDENTITY.

**B**UT MANY COMMUNITIES REMAINED VIBRANT, <u>AND THE JEWISH PEOPLE CONTINUED TO ESTABLISH SPIRITUAL HOMES IN NEW—AND SOMETIMES UNEXPECTED—PLACES.</u>

ASSIMILATING

VIBRANT

HOWEVER, THE MOST INFLUENTIAL DIASPORA COMMUNITY REMAINED...

# THE UNITED STATES

IN THE '40s, HOLLYWOOD SUPPORTED THE WAR EFFORT WITH WAR MOVIES IN WHICH EVERY FOXHOLE SEEMED TO HAVE EVERY KIND OF MINORITY—*ALL DIFFERENT, YET, UNDER FIRE, ALL BRAVE AMERICANS.*

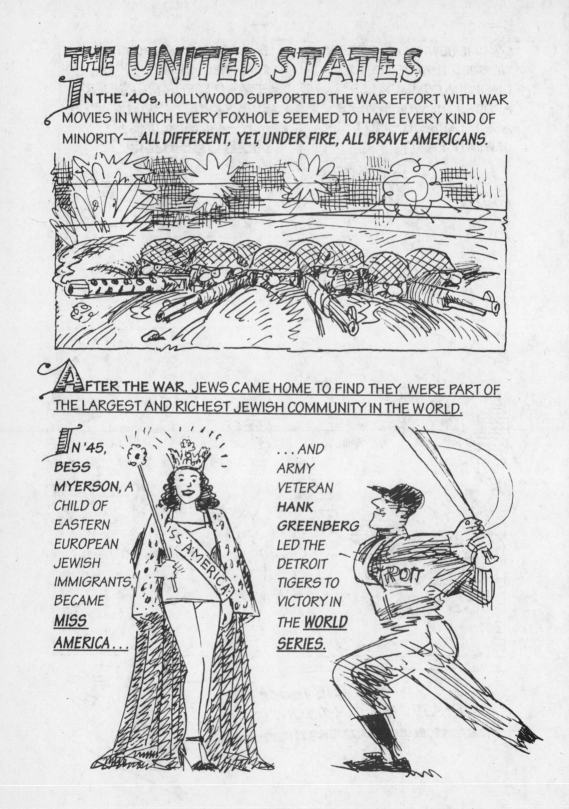

AFTER THE WAR, JEWS CAME HOME TO FIND THEY WERE PART OF THE LARGEST AND RICHEST JEWISH COMMUNITY IN THE WORLD.

IN '45, BESS MYERSON, A CHILD OF EASTERN EUROPEAN JEWISH IMMIGRANTS, BECAME **MISS AMERICA**...

...AND ARMY VETERAN **HANK GREENBERG** LED THE DETROIT TIGERS TO VICTORY IN THE **WORLD SERIES.**

IN THE '60S, THE VALUES OF MIDDLE-CLASS AMERICA CAME UNDER ATTACK FROM THEIR OWN CHILDREN. YOUNG AMERICANS —INCLUDING A TELLING NUMBER OF JEWS—BELIEVED THAT SOCIETY COULD BE IMPROVED THROUGH COMMUNAL ACTION.

FUNNY, OUR CHILDREN DON'T LOOK JEWISH.

THESE YOUNG JEWS FOUND THEIR FAITH IN SOCIAL AND POLITICAL ACTIVISM.

THEY JOINED THE PEACE CORPS AND WENT SOUTH IN THE CIVIL RIGHTS MOVEMENT.

VOTER REGISTRATION

THEY PROTESTED THE WAR IN VIETNAM.

MAKE LOVE NOT WAR!

NG TROOPS HOME

STUDENTS AGAINS

THEIR PROTEST HUMOR, POETRY, AND SONGS RALLIED A GENERATION.

LENNY BRUCE

ALLEN GINSBERG

BOB DYLAN

By 1970, DISSENSION HAD SPLIT APART THE COLLECTIVE MOVEMENTS. THOUGH UNCERTAIN OF THEIR OWN TRADITIONS...

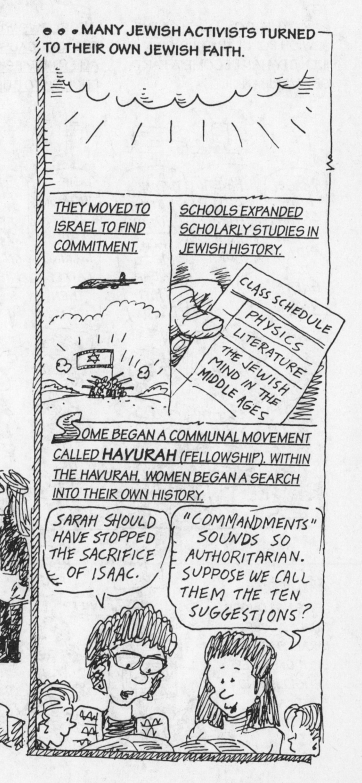

...MANY JEWISH ACTIVISTS TURNED TO THEIR OWN JEWISH FAITH.

THEY MOVED TO ISRAEL TO FIND COMMITMENT.

SCHOOLS EXPANDED SCHOLARLY STUDIES IN JEWISH HISTORY.

CLASS SCHEDULE
PHYSICS
LITERATURE
THE JEWISH MIND IN THE MIDDLE AGES

SOME BEGAN A COMMUNAL MOVEMENT CALLED **HAVURAH** (FELLOWSHIP). WITHIN THE HAVURAH, WOMEN BEGAN A SEARCH INTO THEIR OWN HISTORY.

SARAH SHOULD HAVE STOPPED THE SACRIFICE OF ISAAC.

"COMMANDMENTS" SOUNDS SO AUTHORITARIAN. SUPPOSE WE CALL THEM THE TEN SUGGESTIONS?

259

IN THE 1990s, WITH THE INTERMARRIAGE RATE AT 50%, JEWISH LEADERS WORRIED THAT U.S. JEWRY WAS DISAPPEARING.

THE ORTHODOX BELIEVED THAT STRICT OBSERVANCE WAS THE ONLY WAY JUDAISM WOULD SURVIVE.

WE DIDN'T ASSIMILATE IN BABYLONIA OR GREECE, WE MUST NOT ASSIMILATE HERE!

HASN'T BEEN IN A SYNAGOGUE SINCE HIS BAR MITZVAH.

MARRIED TO A PROTESTANT AND PLANS TO RAISE CHILDREN HALF AND HALF.

ONLY JEWISH OBSERVANCE IS ATTENDING PASSOVER SEDER.

ONLY JEWISH CONNECTION IS ROSH HASHANAH CARD FROM MOTHER.

YOUR NAME ISN'T STAN, IT'S SHLOMO!

GRANDPA?

OY!

AT THE SAME TIME...

...YOUNG JEWS WERE SHOWING A REVITALIZED INTEREST IN THEIR FAITH AND HERITAGE, LINING UP TO JOIN SYNAGOGUES LED BY ENERGETIC YOUNG MALE AND FEMALE RABBIS.

MANY BELIEVED THEY COULD HEAR AND RESPOND TO GOD IN HIS OR HER OWN WAY.

I'M STILL UNCOMFORTABLE TALKING ABOUT GOD, BUT I'VE JOINED A TALMUD STUDY GROUP.

I JUST FEEL GOOD HERE.

I WANT MY CHILDREN TO KNOW MORE THAN I DO.

I'VE JOINED A LESS THEISTIC SYNAGOGUE.

FOR ME, JUDAISM IS A SOCIAL, POLITICAL, AND CULTURAL GLUE THAT BINDS US TOGETHER.

JUDAISM IS ABOUT FINDING GOD IN THE LOGIC OF THE SEASONS.

CONGREGATION MW OGHN
PRAYER
STUDY
SERVICE
FAMILY
USER-FRIENDLY

TRADITIONAL DENOMINATIONS ADJUSTED TO THE CHANGING TIMES. AS IT HAD THROUGH HISTORY, JEWISH DIVERSITY FLOURISHED.

MY REFORM TEMPLE IS GEARED TO SOCIAL ACTION, GENDER EQUALITY, AND A CONTINUING EVOLUTION OF JEWISH TRADITION.

MY CONSERVATIVE SYNAGOGUE IS MODERNIZING CONSERVATIVELY— NEITHER TOO FAR TO THE LEFT, NOR TO THE RIGHT.

WE MODERN ORTHODOX STUDY THE TALMUD ON THE INTERNET, BY SATELLITE, AND ON OUR COMMUTER TRAINS.

IN RECONSTRUCTIONISM, WE PREFER THE COSMIC TO THE SUPERNATURAL. GOD HAS A VOTE, NOT A VETO.

IN OUR JEWISH RENEWAL SERVICES, WE EMPHASIZE JOYOUS DANCE, MEDITATION, POETRY, AND HEALING.

MY SYNAGOGUE IS UNAFFILIATED. OUR MEMBERS HAVE AN EQUAL SAY, ARE NON-IDEOLOGICAL, AND HAVE LOW DUES.

I'M A CULTURAL JEW. FOR ME, JUDAISM IS JUST COMPASSIONATE PEOPLE SEEKING MEANING AND DIGNITY IN LIFE.

And so, Jews around the world—traditional, cultural, and confused—continue their journey, **<u>claiming their portion of a heritage rich in humanity, faith, and achievement.</u>**

THROUGH IT ALL, THE JEWISH PEOPLE CONTINUE TO GATHER TOGETHER AS INDIVIDUALS AND AS FAMILIES, IN CELEBRATION, PRAYER . . . AND ARGUMENT (AGREEING TO DISAGREE)—*AS THEY HAVE SINCE THE DAYS OF ABRAHAM AND SARAH.*

# INDEX

Page numbers in *italics* refer to maps.

## ABOUT THE AUTHOR

The recipient of awards from the American Booksellers Association and the American Institute of Graphic Arts, STAN MACK is a graduate of the Rhode Island School of Design and the former art director of *The New York Times Magazine*. He's created regular cartoon features for *Adweek, Modern Maturity, Print,* and *Natural History,* and *Real Life Funnies* for *The Village Voice.* He's authored and/or illustrated over a dozen children's books and collaborates on young adult books with his partner, Janet Bode.